Dave Phillips's life is an American success story, from disability and ridicule to achievement and acclaim. His journey teaches invaluable lessons to those just starting out and it confirms the truth of freedom's power for us all. He is a good friend; he is also an inspiration.

**Mitt Romney**
Republican Presidential Nominee 2012
Governor of Massachusetts 2003–2007

Dave Phillips served North Carolina as an energetic secretary of commerce who helped me recruit hundreds of thousands of new jobs from all over the world. He's a fireball.

**James B. Hunt Jr.**
Governor of North Carolina 1977–1985, 1993–2001

It has been my honor and pleasure to know and work with Dave Phillips and enjoy his friendship. Dave and Kay and their family have been strong leaders of the business, political, and social life of the Triad region and across North Carolina for many years. To truly understand the will to succeed and the ambition to serve his state and community, you must read *Come On, America* by journalist Mary Bogest. It is within these pages that you will discover and appreciate the spark of determination and inspiration that transformed obstacles into courage and leadership. You will also discover a good and talented writer.

**James G. Martin**
Governor of North Carolina 1985–1993

*Come On, America* is a unique book full of historical, personal, and inspirational gems from the life of my friend Dave Phillips. Whether you know Dave or not you will be impressed and impacted by his life full of challenges, exciting experiences, and gigantic contributions to our world. His growth mindset has driven him to a constant pursuit of success and happiness, truly an outstanding example for all of us.

**Kelly S. King**
Chairman and CEO, BB&T Corporation

Dave Phillips gets things done—against the odds, despite the obstacles, with faith, humor, smarts, and even a little mischief! The world of Special Olympics is lucky to count him as a leader, a friend, and most of all, a believer in the strength and beauty of the human spirit.

**Tim Shriver**

Chairman, Special Olympics


Mary Bogest has created a beautiful and captivating profile in personal courage, persistence, and commitment to service that is the heart and soul of this North Carolinian son, Ambassador Dave Phillips. Far from whining about the serious physical challenges that hobbled his youth, Dave used these very limitations, and the painful setbacks that accompanied them, to shape a truly remarkable life. Prepare to be inspired by the story of a man who has done well and continues to do enormous good for his family, his friends, his state, and his country.

**Dr. Edward J. Shanahan**

Former Headmaster; Choate Rosemary Hall School; Wallingford, CT

Come On America

# Come on
# AMERICA

*The Inspirational Journey of Ambassador*
## DAVE PHILLIPS

## *MARY BOGEST*

NEW YORK

LONDON • NASHVILLE • MELBOURNE • VANCOUVER

# Come On America

## The Inspirational Journey of Ambassador Dave Phillips

Published in New York, New York, by Morgan James Publishing. Morgan James is a trademark of Morgan James, LLC. www.MorganJamesPublishing.com

ISBN 9781683507178 paperback
ISBN 9781683507192 hardcover
ISBN 9781683507185 eBook
Library of Congress Control Number: 2017912593

**Cover Design by:**
Chris Ward

**Interior Design by:**
Chris Treccani
www.3dogcreative.net

Morgan James is a proud partner of Habitat for Humanity Peninsula and Greater Williamsburg. Partners in building since 2006.

Get involved today! Visit
MorganJamesPublishing.com/giving-back

*To my late husband, Stanley, who always believed in me*

*Do what you can with what you have where you are.*
—TEDDY ROOSEVELT

# CONTENTS

# FOREWORD

I f you don't know Dave Phillips, you'll be inspired by his intense determination, his continuous curiosity, and—of course—his personal and professional triumphs. He is no ordinary man. He is an extraordinary catalyst who makes good things happen in business and in life. Serving his community and representing his country.

If you do know Dave Phillips, you'll enjoy reading this book. It will remind you about his life, his work, his family, and his passions. You'll look at the many pictures with admiration and appreciation. You'll be grateful, yet again, that he is your friend, your colleague, and your neighbor.

Mary Bogest is a talented artist and writer who has an extraordinary ability to capture the essence of a subject and communicate it with clarity. This book is an example of what she can do: study the life of an accomplished American and chronicle it in a way that is both captivating and compelling. You'll love her work.

She shows masterful skill and experience in researching the substantive body of data about the life of Ambassador Phillips—and synthesizing it in ways readers will find interesting, inspiring, and informative.

She tells us about the boy who grew up with physical challenges, the man who built successful businesses, the community leader tapped to guide his city's and state's economic development, and the US citizen selected to represent his country as ambassador to Estonia. It's quite a story about a fascinating person whose humility and warmth bring him favor and fortune among family and friends, along with a mass of accolades and a load of distinctive recognitions.

Although this book is biographical, it is also an anecdotal citation that states the facts and, almost unintentionally, creates in the reader the spirited acknowledgment that America is still the land of bountiful opportunity, that you were created by God for a purposeful life, and that it is possible to work hard, enjoy the fruits of your labor, and serve humankind with abundant stewardship.

At High Point University, our goal is to plant seeds of greatness in the minds, hearts, and souls of our students so they can have a life filled with success and framed with significance. Ah, yes, a life filled with success and framed with significance.

That's what you'll conclude when you enjoy this book: Dave Phillips has a life filled with success and framed with significance.

NIDO R. QUBEIN
President, High Point University

# CHAPTER 1

## *An Unexpected Opportunity*

As a featured columnist in the local High Point, North Carolina, newspaper, I had expected my meeting with Dave Phillips to be of a historical nature. High Point has long been synonymous with the furniture industry and is considered to be the "Furniture Capital of the World." Dave Phillips played a significant role in that with his creation of the Market Square Partnership, which had transformed the old Tomlinson furniture manufacturing plant into a fifteen-story, internationally recognized office and home furnishings showroom complex.

I also knew that he had served as the North Carolina secretary of commerce, chairman of the 1999 Special Olympics World Games, and the US ambassador to Estonia. We planned to meet at his office on the tenth floor of Market Square Tower.

On the day of our meeting, I stepped out of the elevator and into an office filled with mementos. I marveled as I sat in the splendid leather chair, waiting for Dave to arrive. Throughout my years as a columnist, I had been in many offices but never had I seen one like this.

A white silk scarf swayed softly in the faint breeze. I recognized it as a khata, the traditional Tibetan scarf. Nearby was the photo of Kay and Dave Phillips in the Himalayas with the Dalai Lama, khatas draped on their wrists, awaiting a blessing. I opened John F. Kennedy's book *Profiles in Courage*. Inside was not only a personalized inscription but a letter from Eunice Shriver signed, "Affectionately, Eunice."

I picked up a dinner invitation. It was from Bill and Hillary Clinton. A birthday card was from George and Laura Bush. The signed Boston Red Sox baseball bat was a gift from Mitt Romney.

My mind raced as I pondered what I would say to him. We had only met a few times before, but as my eyes were filled with wonder, I knew this would be a special meeting.

In a few short minutes, Dave arrived, smiling and effervescent. His long strides barely masked a slightly uneven gait. I had heard that the uneven gait had been due to a difficult challenge while growing up.

During our conversation, Dave talked about Market Square, as well as his life and his family. He had started his own businesses after his father died and then sold three businesses to companies on the New York Stock Exchange. Dave and his wife, Kay, have four grown daughters. The normally ebullient man became reflective as we spoke.

The history of Market Square was undeniable. But I made the decision then and there that even more interesting than the history of the building was the history of the man, the challenges he had faced, and the significant impact he had made in his community, his state, and his nation while pursuing his endeavors in both business and government.

As I was about to leave his office, I noticed an engraved leather sign displayed on his desk with the words "No Whining." It had been a gift from his wife, Kay. It became immediately apparent to me that his personal philosophy—learning life's valuable lessons through highs and lows, ups and downs, without complaining— deserved more than just a feature article in the local paper. It deserved a book.

Could I convince Dave to let me write about his life's journey?

He was at first reluctant. He wasn't eager to share personal details about not only his life but also his family's life and the lives of his business partners, colleagues, and friends. A book about Dave Phillips? It just wasn't him. Besides, who would be interested in it?

He told me he'd think about it.

About three weeks later, I got a call from Dave, and he asked if I could meet him at his office that afternoon. *This was it,* I thought. *The moment of truth.*

As I sat there, feeling a bit nervous, Dave said, "You asked me whether you could write a book about my life and the journey I've been on. Well, I'd like to tell you about an experience I just had."

Dave leaned back in his chair, closed his eyes, and crossed his arms. He told me that he had just returned from his class reunion at Choate, a preparatory high school in Wallingford, Connecticut.

As an active alumnus, having served on the board of trustees, Dave had walked the halls many times at Choate since being a student there over fifty years earlier. But this time was different.

This time, he stopped for a moment in those halls, remembering the boy he once was, the boy who was lucky to get into the prestigious private college-preparatory boarding school that boasted John F. Kennedy as their most famous graduate.

Now, he was returning for his class reunion as a recent recipient of Choate's highest honor, the Choate Rosemary Hall Alumni Award (formerly the Choate Seal). His eyes remained closed as they often would during our meetings as he remembered that weekend.

When Dave attended Choate, it had been an all-male school. That restriction changed when the school, founded in 1898, merged with the all-girls Rosemary Hall School located in Greenwich, Connecticut, in 1971, and it is today known as Choate Rosemary Hall.

I learned Dave was fascinated by architecture from his vivid descriptions of the architecturally diverse buildings on campus. Among the Georgian and Colonial-style buildings stood modern ones, most notably the Paul Mellon Arts Center, a gift from a Choate graduate, Paul Mellon, and designed by I. M. Pei. Dave told me that Pei had later incorporated his design for Choate into the East Building of the National Gallery of Art in Washington, DC.

Over eight hundred alumni from different classes had descended on the campus for Reunion Weekend. Coincidentally, the Choate Class of 1961 had decided on the theme, "Reflecting on Our Lives."

As a recipient of the Alumni Award, Dave was asked to share his introspective thoughts on this theme, along with fellow classmate and Alumni Award recipient Jonathan Fanton. Fanton had served as president of The John D. and Catherine T. MacArthur Foundation, chairman of the board of Human Rights Watch, and president of the New School in New York City.

Dave shared that years earlier, while at Choate, he had been known as a mischief-maker to the point that he was almost permanently kicked out of school. He marveled that this same student, who struggled with academics but excelled in misconduct, would be the recipient of Choate's highest honor. And now he was at his reunion with some of the same classmates who drank with him, smoked with him, and even served as accomplices with him in certain "endeavors." I would learn more about these endeavors later.

During the "Reflection on Our Lives" alumni panel, classmates told of their own challenges and difficulties, which marked lives that had begun with the brightest of promises.

At earlier reunions, classmates would typically show photographs of children and tell stories of business successes, but now that tone had changed dramatically. Their prestigious school's mission was to prepare them for life, and sometimes that life didn't work out as planned.

Panelists spoke of their children and their children's children. Some spoke of the sorrow of losing a child. Dave listened intently to each story. Many had been close friends of his for decades, yet he had never known the depth of their challenges. Their stories were an inspiration and an invitation to truthfully contemplate the meaning of his own challenges.

Later, he sat in silence among an intimate group gathered around a dinner table, raptly listening, until a question was asked directly to him.

"How did you lose your leg?"

Everyone knew Dave had an artificial leg. That had been obvious. Sometimes, as Dave kicked a football, his leg would fly off. It always brought laughter but never questions during those days. Although it was unusual to have an artificial leg back in the 1950s, no one had ever asked him what had happened.

"I was surprised they were so curious," Dave told me. They asked him if he had been in an accident, and he told them, no, he had been born with a birth defect. He added, "As I grew, my left leg did not grow properly above or below the knee. As a child, I had to wear a six-inch built-up shoe. But having a built-up shoe was not the worst thing," he said, laughing. "I could really kick a football. Also, I could hold my own in a fight!"

After countless surgeries, at the age of fourteen, doctors decided to amputate his leg just below the knee. Right about that time, he entered Choate.

"It was really wonderful for me to go off to Choate because I wasn't unusual. I went to Choate with an artificial leg—but it was a leg. I no longer walked with crutches or a built-up shoe. It was a whole new life, and I have always been grateful," Dave had told his classmates.

Dave opened his eyes and sat forward. "I've been reflecting a lot on that weekend," he told me. "I began to think about the stories and reflections I want to pass on, not just to my classmates but also to my four daughters and to their children."

He paused and looked directly at me. "I'm willing to share my story with you, but only if it could help others find success in their stories. I wouldn't want them to look at my life and feel like they had to own a business or become an ambassador in order to be successful. To me, success means going to sleep at night thinking about what happened that day and feeling satisfied that you have done all you could do."

Of course, I agreed. Although I was ecstatic that former US ambassador, Dave Phillips, this man who had led such a unique and meaningful life, would allow me to write my first book about him, I knew his life story would be inspirational to far more than just his children. I could already list in my head so many people who would benefit from seeing how he had overcome his physical and academic challenges to create his prosperous business ventures and become a respected leader representing his state and his nation around the world.

But I had a question I wasn't sure how to ask.

"You and I both know that money alone doesn't make you successful. You had to overcome a handicap, a leg amputation, bullying, and more. I think the first thing readers will want to know is, how did you do it? How were you able to achieve that kind of success, while others in similar circumstances struggle?"

Dave pondered again. "Attitude," he said. "I think the reason I could get through each of those obstacles was that I had just enough of a taste of success to get me to the next opportunity."

Now I was really intrigued. "What do you mean?"

He smiled. "Let me try to explain."

Over the next many months, we would meet in Dave's office, always face to face, as he insisted. Our meetings would be sporadic as often he would be traveling with Kay, visiting their children.

I was awe-inspired at the opportunity to write my first book. I also felt honored, very honored. Yet, I knew this was an even greater opportunity for those who haven't met Dave Phillips personally, particularly those facing what may seem like impossible obstacles, whether it's a physical handicap, illness, catastrophe, business failure, job loss, addiction, or lost relationship.

I can't say it is my persuasive finesse that got Dave to agree for me to write this book. It is really about timing. It is about history.

My hope is that as you're inspired by Dave Phillips's life, as I was, you will discover your path to success and allow it to take you to your next opportunity, and the next, and the next.

# CHAPTER 2

# A Taste of Success

One week later, I arrived for our first meeting. Dave and I sat at a mahogany leather-top table, as we would for all our meetings, next to sweeping, fifteen-foot-high windows overlooking the city of High Point. It was a clear day, and our view extended all the way to Pilot Mountain, forty miles away.

As soon as we began, I could tell that I had just embarked on a fascinating adventure. Dave was very charming, and we spent the first thirty minutes chatting about what had happened in town that week.

Now there was the question of where to begin. And that answer was, simply, at the beginning—with his childhood.

"You can see the schools I went to from here," Dave said, pointing out the window to the distant adjacent elementary, middle, and high schools.

"As a child, I remember one particular friend who had an attic, and she put together a neighborhood gang. It's funny to think we called them 'gangs' back then. We had a gang initiation rite that I have never forgotten. You had to swallow an oyster that was tied to a string, and then they would pull it up by the string. I've never liked oysters since!

7

"In general, my parents were very good at including my brother Phil and me with older people. If they had a party or a function, they wanted us to come say hello to the guests. My father had a lot of parties for the furniture industry, where people from all over America came to High Point, and I was able, especially as a teenager, to get to know these people.

"But even earlier, I remember going to many parties where there were just my parents' friends, so I think being introduced to older people at a young age made me feel more comfortable with people throughout my life."

He paused. "At the same time, I always knew I was odd because I had a birth defect."

Dave told me that when he was born, his left foot pointed forty-five degrees outward (versus a club foot, he explained, that usually turns inward at forty-five degrees), and he had only three toes.

"For me, this sense of being odd was simply part of growing up. I knew people were curious, and somehow, I just learned to deal with it. I remember playing with the neighborhood children and how the girls would ask to count my toes. How fascinated they were—they thought I had the cutest toes!"

He underwent numerous surgeries throughout his childhood to try to correct the defect.

"First, they worked on my foot, slowly trying to straighten it. Then they worked on my knee and ankle. They finally figured out that my left thigh was not growing as fast as my right thigh, and there was considerable concern about the unevenness of my knees. My left lower leg eventually stopped growing completely, and I began wearing a two-inch, then a four-inch, and finally a six-inch built-up shoe.

"Through all this time, my mother drove me back and forth to the doctor in Charlotte. Back then, there were no super highways, and I remember that she always stopped at the Howard Johnson on the way home, where they had twenty-eight flavors of ice cream, and she let me order whatever ice cream I wanted."

The shoe was made of balsa wood, Dave said, because of its light weight, and covered in leather. But it still caused a noticeable limp, which meant Dave could not participate in sports like his schoolmates.

"It's amazing that, looking back at it, I don't have horrible memories of growing up. Now, there were bullies. There weren't any in my neighborhood, but once I started first grade at the elementary school, I encountered a new level of scrutiny, and that was hard. I had this big, built-up shoe, and I couldn't play most sports, so I was different than most kids."

Once he got to junior high, however, the bullying increased.

"That was a whole new level of scrutiny," Dave explained. "But I learned to fight back when I had to, especially with that shoe, and eventually I gained their respect. I'll never forget one guy. He and I would get into fights all the time, and one time I kicked him as hard as I could with my built-up shoe.

"After that happened, I got the reputation that you'd better be careful around me because I was a pretty good fighter with that leg," Dave laughed.

"So, you learned to deal with the bullies," I said.

"Actually, what I remember most about junior high was developing rheumatic heart disease and being confined for four months on the second story of our house."

Dave explained that, at that time, rheumatic fever had caused thousands of deaths, especially in children. It was more than serious; it could have been deadly. There was no known cure, and the only treatment was high doses of penicillin to control the symptoms.

He took an enormous amount of penicillin, but even that wasn't enough. The doctors at the time said the disease was possibly contagious, and therefore, the patient should remain isolated and avoid all exercise and stress.

"I wasn't even allowed to go downstairs because of the supposed stress on my heart. During the day, I would stay in my parents' bedroom watching television, and it was a great diversion. To this day, I remember *Art Linkletter's House Party* came on every afternoon at three o'clock. The highlight of the show was the segment 'Kids Say the Darndest Things.'

"But in the early 1950s, most people did not even own a television, and very few shows were on television at the time, especially during the daytime. I was growing restless.

"Most of whom I watched on television was Gene Autry and Roy Rogers, who had pistols and gun holsters. I still can't believe to this day what my mother did. I guess she felt sorry for me. She bought me a pistol—an authentic .22-caliber revolver pistol that even had a bullet holster that fastened around the waist, just like on television.

"How many parents give their child a gun when they're twelve?" Dave wondered, shaking his head. "I was so excited; I couldn't stand it.

"My mother would put a paper bullseye target on a tree, and I'd go out on the porch and fire away! That was one good thing about being surrounded by woods—no one would get hurt."

One day, while Dave was on the upstairs porch shooting paper targets tacked to a tree, he saw their gardener, Pee Wee, walking by carrying a large, empty glass jar. McKinley Simms (called Pee Wee because of his small stature) lived in a log cabin nestled in the Phillips's wooded property and was particularly fond of Dave.

Dave and Pee Wee started talking, and Dave said, "Pee Wee, would you hold that jar out so I can shoot it?"

Surprisingly, Pee Wee obliged. He held out the empty jar at arm's length, holding on to the screw top with his fingers and covering his eyes.

"I took a downward aim, pulled the trigger, and I was so excited to see the glass fly. At the time, I thought it was the greatest thing. Then I asked Pee Wee if he had any more jars, and I shot a few more," Dave said.

Every few days, when Dave's mother was out running errands or at the grocery store, he and Pee Wee would reenact the same scene. While Pee Wee was very good at picking up all of the glass, it wasn't long before Dave's mother discovered some broken shards he had missed.

"All of a sudden, my mother was inquiring about the glass in the backyard and the story came out. She got very upset and so did my dad. They took my pistol away and told Pee Wee that he could never do that again," he recalled. Dave said he has had nightmares over the years just imagining what could have happened to Pee Wee.

Although Pee Wee was able to elude the bullets fired by Dave, years later he would not be so fortunate eluding the long arm of the law. I learned that the log cabin Pee Wee lived in on the property was used for much more than sleeping. He was arrested for bootlegging, selling moonshine in mason jars. When Pee

Wee was charged with a federal offense, Dave's father hired the best trial lawyer in town to defend his gardener. Since Pee Wee was caught with "the goods," he had no choice but to plead guilty.

"Pee Wee's sentencing was scheduled in December, shortly before Christmas," Dave said. "The judge told him, 'You are being sent to federal prison in either Pennsylvania or Florida.' Pee Wee answered simply, 'Judge, I'd rather go south for the winter.' So, Pee Wee spent about three months in the federal prison in Florida and then came back to the family."

Years later, Dave said, Pee Wee died of natural causes, and he attended his funeral. Dave went up to the open casket, and Pee Wee's hands were folded on his chest. "I put my hands on his and said a prayer: 'Pee Wee, thank goodness I never hit you or wounded you or maimed you. Thank you, Pee Wee, for being my friend when I needed you.'"

Dave smiled at the memory of Pee Wee. Then we returned to twelve-year-old Dave, stuck on the second floor without his pistol.

"What did you do after your pistol was taken away?" I asked.

"Not long after that, my dad and some of his friends took me to a skeet field. I started shooting skeet, which are small, round clay discs thrown in the air by a machine.

"There was one man named Horace Ilderton . . . Here, I think I have a picture of him."

Dave stood up and started scanning the framed pictures that covered his office walls; he lifted one off its nail and handed it to me. It was a picture of Dave at age twelve with his built-up shoe, aiming at a target, and an older gentleman in his sixties, hands folded over his gun, looking on.

"Mr. Ilderton died a long time ago, but he was just a wonderful personality in the neighborhood, and he loved to shoot. He took an interest in me. A whole bunch of men like that were all mentors to me. Here I was, this twelve-year-old kid, walking around with these men in their fifties or sixties, and they learned to trust me with a gun. So, that's another way I learned to get along with older people at a young age."

He sat back down in his chair, leaned back, and thought for a moment.

"I'd say that's when I had my first taste of success, when those men took an interest in me and I realized I was good at shooting. They took me to competitions, and I started winning awards and traveling to tournaments. I continued that all through junior high and high school and even into college. I think knowing I was really good at something, no matter how small, was what helped me get through those tough years."

I was curious to know more about what he meant and asked him to explain.

Dave paused, then said thoughtfully, "Knowing I could do something successfully gave me confidence. That's the true key to success: having the confidence that you've already done something successfully, so you can do it again.

"That's why I tell people who are going through a hard time to look for that taste of success, something they can build on. What are you good at? What do you like to do? Go do that, and focus on that—not on the things that aren't going right. That taste of success can carry you right through until the next opportunity, which might be right around the corner, as it was for me. It can give you the confidence that, even though you may be facing a huge challenge, you can overcome it because you've been successful before."

# CHAPTER 3

# *You Don't Have Enemies, You Have Opposition*

Dave told me more about those tough years. As much as he excelled in skeet shooting, he did not excel in his studies. Missing many months of school didn't help; however, he did have a tutor, Mrs. Hunt Moffitt, who was a friend of the family. Dave looked forward to her visits several times a week, although he did say he found it amusing that Mrs. Moffitt was also the tutor for mentally challenged students in the High Point City School System!

Though those months felt like years, the rheumatic fever finally dissipated, and Dave could once again go outside.

The summer before he started high school, Dave and his mother were driving home from yet another doctor's visit in Charlotte related to his leg. They had gotten ice cream at the Howard Johnson as usual, and when they got back into the car, Dave's mother turned toward him and said something he would never forget.

"My mother explained to me that the doctors thought it was best to stop trying to fix my leg and to amputate it below the knee," Dave said. "Amputating below the knee was much better than losing the knee, she said, because it would make recovery and fitting the artificial leg easier.

"Then she looked me in the eyes and told me, 'If they do amputate, we'll let you get any style of shoe you want,' knowing I had been wearing the same style of shoe for fourteen years."

Tears sprang to my eyes. "It sounds like your mother was an incredibly positive person," I said quietly.

"She was. She was always so encouraging and helped me focus on the future, no matter what. That summer, I went to Charlotte Memorial Hospital for the surgery to amputate my lower leg."

"I'm so sorry," I said, imagining how traumatic it must have been for a fourteen-year-old boy to lose his leg.

"I was actually relieved," said Dave.

"Really?" I said, shocked.

"My leg had been a problem since I was born. The prospect of me being normal was exciting. The man who cut off my leg, Dr. Carr, was a noted surgeon during the war, and he had performed many, many amputations. So, my parents felt secure, as did I."

So, there was Dave, a young teenager on the operating table at Charlotte Memorial Hospital, relieved to be losing his leg. But to him, it didn't mean the loss of freedom or ability. It meant the end of disappointing surgeries, crutches, physical pain, and the built-up shoe—and the beginning of normalcy.

I must not have looked convinced that losing his leg wasn't traumatic for him, so he told me another story.

"I had been known to sneak out for a smoke," he said, "which was pretty common at that time. A friend of mine had sent a floral arrangement to my hospital room, and it really caught my eye. This floral arrangement had cigarettes sticking out of the middle, and it was placed on a table across the room from my bed.

"Now, how would I, with one leg, cross the room to get to the cigarettes? Well, I was dumb enough to try to get out of bed myself. I fell on my stump, and the doctors thought they would have to operate again because I had split some of the sutures. You'd think that would have stopped me from ever smoking, but I'm sorry to say it didn't!"

After the amputation, Dave was fitted with a hollow metal leg. But his leg needed to heal before he could use the artificial leg, so he spent quite a few months getting around on crutches.

That was also when he started ninth grade at the local high school, and the bullying and taunts escalated even further.

"Senior high covered a lot more of High Point," Dave explained. "Kids came in from all over the town, including 'across the tracks,' as they used to call it. Ours was a manufacturing town, so you lived on one side or the other. So, now there were even more people whom I never knew or who didn't know me, and that's why I was such a target," he explained.

William, who worked for the Phillips family during the week, would often drive Dave to school, especially after his operation.

"What I remember most about William was that he was a fabulous whistler. He taught me how to whistle on our way to school in the car. Even today when I whistle, I think of William," recalled Dave.

"I loved William; he was part of our family. He was also a minister of one of High Point's churches. He taught me a prayer that I memorized, and to this day, it's the only prayer I know. Can I share it with you?"

"Of course," I said.

*Our Father in Heaven,*
*We thank Thee for food, shelter, and friends.*
*Help us to be true to Thee and ourselves.*
*In Christ's name,*
*Amen*

While at school, Dave carried his books in an army-green cotton satchel and would attach it to his crutches. The school bullies saw this as an opportunity and would regularly knock the crutches out from under Dave, spilling his books all over the floor.

Yet, Dave's father's friends also took him out skeet shooting as soon as he was able, and Dave took great joy in excelling at the sport. He remembers sitting on a stool with one leg while taking aim and shooting in Roaring Gap, in the North Carolina Blue Ridge Mountains.

"Here, let me show you something," said Dave as he got up and brought back a copy of an article from the 1956 *Charlotte News and Observer* with the headline, "High Point Boy's Courage Impresses Skeet Shooters." I read,

> A 14-year-old High Point lad who had his leg amputated two months ago is back on the skeet range—banging birds as usual. Dave Phillips' left leg has always been shorter than his right and building a left shoe to keep him upright was a growing problem. Doctors advised his father, Earl Phillips, that a leg amputation six inches below the knee would make it easier to fit the lad with a limb as he grew and would eliminate the cumbersome shoe. "Let's amputate," said Dave. The operation in Charlotte Memorial Hospital by Drs. Oscar Miller and Carr was successful. Dave got back on the skeet range two weeks ago. Last weekend, at the old High Point range, where he learned to shoot under Jack Holbrook and Seborn Perry, he broke 50 straight birds. His father took him to Roaring Gap and on the Graystone Inn's skeet range, young Dave shot 56 straight, missed one, and then went on straight for 74 out of 75 birds. The next day he cracked 25 straight, making 99 out of 100. All told he has shot 12 straight 50s. He sits on a tripod seat and knocks down the birds with the coolness of a veteran. Dave, who learned most of his shooting at Seagull Camp, is an NRA Ranger and NRA Marksman 1st Class (Junior Division). Gunners who have watched him in action think it is a miracle of courage.

"Amazing," I said, impressed.

"I still take my family and friends to that same skeet field at Roaring Gap."

"So, you mentioned that skeet shooting was the 'taste of success' that helped you endure all those challenges you faced during childhood and junior high. Are there any other lessons you learned from that time in your life?"

Dave thought a moment. "Well, I did learn some valuable lessons from those bullies. I learned how to take taunts. I learned to survive. I learned not to get riled up, but when things reach a certain point, it's better to fight back.

"I also learned that people mature. Later, you might find yourselves acknowledging each other instead of fighting each other, and then you just might get to know each other.

"That guy who I kicked with my built-up shoe in junior high—I ran into him at the furniture market in High Point twenty-five or thirty years ago. I saw him walking down the hall toward me, and I recognized him right away. He started smiling, and I started smiling, too. He came over to me, and he couldn't have been friendlier or happier to see me. And I've seen him several times since.

"The truth is, we don't have enemies; we have opposition. I learned that at an early age, and I carried that lesson with me throughout my life."

# CHAPTER 4

# *The Accidental Yankee*

After his bout with rheumatic fever and undergoing the surgery to amputate his lower leg, Dave's parents decided that instead of returning to the local school for the tenth grade, going off to a boarding school would be the best thing for him. Not just to avoid bullies, he clarified, but to give him a better education. Phil had already gone off to Woodberry Forest in Virginia, so the idea of going to boarding school wasn't unexpected.

However, Dave's father had a very good friend from Greensboro named Harry Carter, who had moved to New York to run a large textile company, and Harry told Dave's father he was sending his son to a prep school called Choate in Connecticut.

Although it wasn't unusual for a Southern boy to go away to a boarding school in those days, apparently it was unusual for a Southern boy to attend a "Yankee" boarding school. Nevertheless, based solely on this friend's recommendation, his parents immediately took him for a visit and an interview.

Surprisingly, Dave was accepted on that same day, but not without conditions.

"It was a Saturday morning, and I can remember exactly where I was standing: it was in the Paul Mellon Library. They said to me, 'You are accepted now if you come to summer school. We will re-evaluate you after the summer term. Your test scores are not very good, and we will let you know after that,'" Dave recalled.

He did go to summer school and then got the final judgment: his reading and writing skills were poor. He would be accepted only if he would go back one year in school. His parents readily accepted the condition, excited that their son would have an opportunity to go to Choate. Dave was totally embarrassed but did not have a choice.

Later, Dave would say that this turned out to be the best thing that could have happened to him. He admittedly was immature and not well educated and couldn't compete. "I wasn't very good at reading and writing, and they made that very clear." Yet, they still gave him a chance.

Choate was a new start. Where he had been "different" at his hometown high school, here at Choate he was not bullied. He was no longer the boy with the crutches or the built-up shoe; from the outside, he looked no different than anyone else.

"I went off to Choate as a whole new person—a normal person. I felt Choate accepted me the way I was, even though I was held back a year. It was the most valuable four years of my life. I have always been grateful for the opportunity to go to Choate. It was a sanctuary for me."

Even though he couldn't play traditional sports, he was still very involved.

"They made me assistant manager of different sports teams, like football and wrestling. I went to all the games and traveled to all the tournaments, and I felt I was a part of a team for the first time."

Also, Choate had its own skeet field, and the director of athletics would take the students out shooting. Dave would excel in the sport and become captain of the Choate skeet team.

The boys at Choate wore sport coats and ties and went to chapel every evening before dinner. "We were told what to participate in and what classes to take. At the end of every quarter, grades were posted on the bulletin board. You knew who was first and last in your class. My friends and I were always mortified because we were often near the bottom. The only consolation was that they always said that Jack Kennedy, who was the president at the time, had been near the bottom of his class at Choate, so that gave us great comfort."

At Choate, the boys lived in different houses or small dormitories with schoolmasters. Dave's first roommate was from the exclusive Chicago suburb of Lake Forest. When they first met, the upscale Chicagoan was less than impressed as he had never heard of High Point, North Carolina.

"Back in the '50s, there weren't a lot of guys from the South at Choate, and he probably thought he was rooming with a hick."

Dave, and many of his friends, traveled to Choate by train. At that time, traveling by passenger train was very common throughout the United States. The train that came through High Point traveled the famous Old Southern Railway, picking up passengers along the way, including a few of his fellow classmates. From High Point, it was an overnight ride to New York City, continuing on to Wallingford. "This was the most exciting thing that could happen," Dave remembered. "You felt like a grown-up taking the train all the way to New York City. You would have fantasies that something intriguing and mysterious would happen on the train, though nothing ever did."

Although mystery and intrigue did not develop on the train ride, there was plenty of conspiracy and plotting on how and where to get cigarettes and liquor while in New York City. The train's New York City destination was Pennsylvania Station on Manhattan's West Side. The connecting train to Choate was at the Grand Central Station Terminal on the East Side. At Grand Central, the Connecticut-bound train had a special car for the boys going to Choate. The boys' afternoon journey from the West Side to the East Side would provide plenty of opportunities.

Dave remembers one adventure in particular. He and several classmates were sitting in the Rough Rider Room of the Roosevelt Hotel near Grand Central Station and ordered drinks. The knowing bartender adroitly asked the boys for their identification. The boys gladly obliged with their fake IDs. Off the hook for serving minors, the bartender asked the boys for their drink of choice. The boys, trying to prove they were suave and debonair, ordered martinis, the "in" drink at the time. The bartender, probably smirking, asked the boys if they would like that "dry, or extra dry." Of course, they said, "Extra dry." The martinis were extra dry, but within minutes, the boys were not—they were outside Grand Central Station throwing up!

Once the train arrived in Wallingford, the boys would unload their luggage from the train and then walk a few blocks to the school.

While at Choate, Dave was not a particularly good student, and as "boys will be boys," he got into a bit of trouble. At Choate, rules were rules, and they were not to be broken.

"In fact, when I was visiting Choate last week, I told them this story: We were all required to attend chapel every afternoon at five, as well as the service on Sunday. Believe it or not, I was an acolyte, so on Sundays I'd be in my robe with the other acolytes, and we would go down the aisle and assist with communion. There were several bottles of wine downstairs where we changed into our robes, and there was also a hole in the wall where we would pour the wine out and into the ground. Of course, when the service was over, we guys had to have a few cups of wine and toast each other!"

Dave pushed the limit throughout his four years at Choate. He received warnings, was forbidden from going downtown, and was even restricted to campus over one Thanksgiving and could not meet his parents after they had already traveled to New York City.

Dave was very creative in his strategic plans to outmaneuver the rules, and his antics were almost nonstop. One plan of action began on the golf course. As a sports activity, Dave tried out for the junior varsity golf team. His idea was to hit the ball into the woods lining the fairways so he could puff on his cigarettes. Dave also recalled a violation when, as he went to meet with the dean of students, a pack of Marlboro cigarettes was seen prominently in his pocket. Before the meeting began, the dean said to Dave, "Before we talk, take those cigarettes out of your pocket."

He was also known as the distributing agent for alcohol on campus. To his friends, he was known as the "bootlegger," as he used his hollow leg to transport half pints of Johnny Walker Scotch onto campus.

Also, as a classmate recently reminded him, Dave was the "purveyor of penicillin on campus" as he continued to refill his prescription left over from his earlier bout of rheumatic heart disease. They recollected that Dave would supply pills to classmates who had gone into New York and were possibly exposed to diseases from ladies of the night. "They were scared that they had caught something bad and were always grateful that I was generous with my pills," added Dave.

Not all of Dave's fun required breaking the rules. While at Choate, one of the school's masters would take the boys pheasant hunting in the woods around the Connecticut school.

"I still remember carrying my shotgun on the train all the way from High Point to Pennsylvania Station and then walking through New York City to catch the train to Choate at Grand Central. Can you imagine this happening today?"

One memorable summer after his sophomore year, Dave lived in Mexico and attended classes at the University in Guadalajara in the city known as Mexico's "City of Roses." Dave and his roommate lived above a bar with little or no supervision from the host parents. They would travel by bus to the campus every day.

The lack of supervision inspired the teen to do something very unusual back then, and that was to grow a beard.

After spending most of the summer in Mexico, Dave returned to High Point. He hadn't told his parents that he had grown a beard. In those days, the passengers disembarked by walking down the plane's stairway onto the tarmac to the terminal. Dave's parents anxiously awaited their son's arrival. One by one, the passengers stepped off the plane, but Dave's parents did not see their son.

"My mother was looking past me when I walked up to her. She didn't recognize me. I looked at my mother and said, 'Hi, Mom,' and she started crying—definitely not tears of joy but tears of horror. Needless to say, dinner that night was very difficult. I was told to shave my beard off before breakfast, and, of course, I did."

But Dave was about to push the limits to the breaking point. As a senior, Dave was elected chairman of the committee for the annual Choate Winter Black Tie Dance. When a stockpile of liquor was discovered in his care before the dance, and after such a long list of infractions, Headmaster Seymour St. John had to take drastic steps.

Although the headmaster used the word "suspension" rather than "expulsion" when handing out the punishment, it was still a troubling pronouncement: in the winter of his senior year, Dave would have to transfer to another school for four months and graduate from that school. It would be then, and only then, that Dave would be allowed to return to Choate to graduate and receive his diploma.

"My parents were extremely upset and disappointed," said Dave. "I was horrified and embarrassed, and I have never forgotten it. I didn't have the opportunity to return home. I went directly to the Hatch School in Newport, Rhode Island."

His date for the evening was planning to travel to Connecticut from North Carolina, and he had to call her and cancel. Dave would not be able to attend the dance nor participate in any of the dance festivities.

Even so, Dave managed to focus on the positive as he told me about Hatch: "The buildings of the school were mansions of a bygone era, overlooking the sea. My room was on the second floor and had a great view of the water. I introduced myself to my suitemates, and they were very welcoming. At the time, I did not realize that one of them was the great grandson of Henry Ford. He has recently died, but I remain friends with his sister, who is a neighbor of ours in Florida.

"I did graduate from Hatch and was able to return to Choate, where I was very proud and excited to graduate from as well.

"I am probably the only person you know who has two high school diplomas," said Dave, smiling.

"You're right; you are." We laughed as I added, "So, did you have to do another year at Choate, or did they just allow you to walk for graduation?"

"I came back to Choate after graduating from Hatch, and they wanted me to attend a summer program before receiving my diploma. Choate had great summer programs, and I enrolled in the Soviet Studies Program."

# CHAPTER 5

# The Soviet Studies Program

Dave returned to Choate in June of 1961. Choate alumnus President Kennedy had been trying to develop a relationship with Russia, believing that an understanding of the Soviet Union was essential to America's future. The Choate headmaster shared this view, and the summer Soviet Studies Program had been created. In an introductory seminar, students would study the Russian language, Russian history, and Russian current affairs. Then they would travel to the Soviet Union.

It was expected that, at the end of the seminar, the boys would have limited Russian language skills for the most rudimentary of conversations. Yet, the Americans would not be traveling in Russia alone. The Russians stipulated that a government (a.k.a. Communist) agent must accompany them wherever they went, whether by plane, train, or boat. Ludmilla was the Russian agent assigned to the young Americans. In light of this particular caveat, it was hoped that the teenage group would mix with the Russian people more than what was usually permitted for ordinary tourists.

Further, the Russian government requested that the Soviet Studies Program be a coed experience. Both males and females from the United States would travel to Russia. Since Choate at that time was an all-boys school, to abide by the request, two girls from Texas joined the entourage. The female students required a female chaperone on their Russian adventure. Their chaperone, Miss Harris, was in her late twenties, and Dave said everyone thought the smart, attractive chaperone was just fabulous.

So, eight boys and two girls, plus the chaperones, set off on the excursion to Russia. But Dave's mother was still concerned for her son—even with the chaperones. Dave said, "My mother was really scared that I would do something stupid and end up in Siberia."

"It sounds like she had good reason," I laughed.

The students visited some classes at Moscow State University before traveling around the Soviet Union to cities such as Kiev, the capital of Ukraine. They also visited Yalta, the site of the famous World War II Yalta Conference, where Franklin Delano Roosevelt, Joseph Stalin, and Winston Churchill famously met.

It was while in Yalta that one of their most memorable yet innocent escapades occurred. The water in their hotel was not working. This was in the days before bottled water. There was no juice, no liquid of any kind, with the exception of the Russian beverage of choice—vodka. There were plenty of bottles of vodka everywhere, so Miss Harris and the boys substituted the water with vodka to brush their teeth!

They traveled by ship from Yalta on the Black Sea to Tbilisi, the capital of Georgia, then on to Stalingrad, now called Volgograd. They also visited Sochi, the site of the 2014 Winter Olympics, and then toured Leningrad, now called St. Petersburg, which Dave called "the most beautiful and historic city of all."

Throughout the Russian trip, the boys tried to be mindful of the warning given to them when briefed by the State Department.

"This was a highly unusual trip at the time, and the State Department had concerns because we were teenagers. They told us there was a distinct possibility that we would be tempted along the way to test our morals. Just think of the propaganda value if the students from the same school that the president attended were caught in some mischief! Just the previous year, American Gary Powers had been shot down over the Soviet Union while flying a U-2 spy plane on a covert surveillance mission."

Temptations for mischief abounded, even in Russia. The State Department told the boys that if "certain ladies" tried to seduce them, flirt with them, or tempt them, most likely it would be a "set up" and to be extremely aware that it might be a covert action. They could be filmed or recorded. At the time, the social mores in the Soviet Union were far different than the looser morals of the Western world. "Elvis the Pelvis" Presley and his gyrating hips had, by some accounts, rocked the Western world. At the time, the reputation of the United States in the Soviet Union, led by Nikita Khrushchev, was delicate, and it was now in the hands of ten American teenagers.

Their warnings proved to be justified.

While the boys were in their hotel room in Stalingrad, the telephone rang. A female with a low, raspy voice said, "Why don't you come down and visit me?" For a moment, the boys forgot the warning given to them by the State Department.

"Being boys, we thought this was very exciting. We looked at each other and just started to laugh, as if to say, 'Isn't this amazing?' Wisely, none of us accepted the offer."

The State Department had given the boys another warning. On the streets, many Russians were selling black-market Russian Eastern Orthodox icons, which were beautiful Byzantine-style paintings on wood.

"The icons had been stolen from churches and were considered to be treasures of Russia, so they had been nationalized by the Russian government," Dave explained. "We had been told not to buy these icons."

This time the boys did not heed the advice of the State Department. The temptation was just far too great.

"I and another boy just had to have these Russian treasures, so we traded our highly sought-after American blue jeans and Marlboro cigarettes for four icons, two for each of us."

Dave and his friend thought they had gotten a tremendous bargain in their shrewd deal making. Blue jeans and cigarettes were commonly available in the United States but to get four authentic Russian icons—that was a real deal. The icons were not large and could easily fit into a suitcase. The challenge, of course, was smuggling them out of the country. Under any circumstances, that would not be easy, and they were in Communist Russia.

The boys began to rethink their decision making. But what was done was done. Now it was time to figure out their own covert mission—safely getting the treasures of Russia out of the country. This mission had intrigue, peril, and adventure—but how would they do it?

After musing upon their options for some time, the boys finally told Mr. Johannes von Strahlen, the director of the program and the boys' chaperone, exactly what they had done. He was in disbelief and more than a bit horrified.

"You could get into serious trouble for this," he reprimanded them.

"I have a plan to get the icons out of Russia," Dave told von Strahlen.

"How are you going to do that?" he asked.

While on international travels with his parents, Dave had learned a valuable lesson: custom officials do not like to touch an artificial leg. And he just happened to have a spare leg in his luggage.

Dave explained to von Strahlen and his friends that they could hide the icons under his extra leg in his suitcase, and the custom officials would be very unlikely to find them.

The plan sounded like a good one. It really didn't matter; it was the only plan they had. Would it work with the Soviet custom officials?

Unbelievably, and very impressively, everything went according to plan at the Moscow Airport. The suitcases were laid side by side, ready for inspection. One by one, the customs official opened each suitcase and felt around. The stern-looking, militaristic custom official looked at Dave and then methodically opened up his suitcase. The judgment would be either Siberia or America. When the customs official slammed the suitcase shut without touching anything, the escapade literally became a "closed case."

Dave had escaped Siberia after all and arrived back home safely. Later, when Dave confessed to his parents the origin of the icons, they decided that if their young son had succeeded in smuggling priceless Russian icons into the United States, then perhaps they should have them appraised and insured. They took them to Armand Hammer, an industrialist and philanthropist who had developed close ties with the Soviet Union. Through his extensive travels in

Russia, he had become an expert in Russian art. His appreciation of art led him to found the Hammer Gallery in New York, which was the first in the West to exhibit the Russian Imperial Easter Eggs by Carl Faberge. Unfortunately, the art appraiser informed the Phillips that the icons were not worth much. The priceless smuggled treasure was not priceless after all! The icons were very beautiful, just not valuable.

This would not be the last time Dave would hear about Miss Harris or that their paths would cross. Many years later, while she was the headmistress at the exclusive Madeira School for Girls in McLean, Virginia, Miss Harris would gain national headlines. She was "Jean Harris, notorious killer of her philandering boyfriend, cardiologist Dr. Herman Tarnower," and referred to by the media as the "spurned-woman-turned-vengeful killer." Adding to the sensationalism was the fact that Dr. Tarnower had written a best-selling diet book, *The Complete Scarsdale Medical Diet*. The 1980 murder of the popular doctor by his lover rapidly became a high-profile case capturing worldwide media attention.

When reading the stories of the murder of the playboy doctor and the woman who was accused of murdering him, Dave soon realized that the notorious Jean Harris was the same Miss Harris who had been so nice and so much fun in Russia.

Remembering the kind and spunky chaperone, Dave sent money for her legal defense. Harris was convicted of second-degree murder and imprisoned at the Bedford Hills Correctional Facility in Westchester County, New York.

"When she was sent to prison, I wrote letters to her," Dave said. "She wrote back, even talking about our escapade in Yalta in the Crimea. This is also part of the Ukraine, which was just forcibly annexed by Russia in 2014."

He recalled that, while in prison, Harris wrote letters on personalized engraved stationery. "Imagine that—in prison. That was her style."

After arriving in New York City from Moscow, however, Dave discovered his adventure was not quite over.

"Both of my parents were at the airport to greet me. 'We have been invited to go to Washington,' they said. 'We are going on the presidential yacht, the *Honey Fitz,* and we are going right now!'"

# CHAPTER 6

# *The* Honey Fitz

"The presidential yacht?" I asked, completely engrossed.

"Well, we had been invited by Luther Hodges, secretary of commerce under President Kennedy, former governor of North Carolina, and one of my father's best friends."

I learned that the Phillips and the Hodges had originally become friends through the textile industry. Hodges met Earl Phillips, Dave's father, while working at Carolina Cotton and Woolen Mills in Leaksville, North Carolina, and had worked his way up to executive positions with the company. That company was eventually sold to Marshall Field & Company in Chicago. Hodges retired from the industry to get involved in politics and was elected lieutenant governor of North Carolina in 1952. He unexpectedly became governor of North Carolina two years later when Governor William B. Umstead died, and Hodges had become a very popular and beloved politician.

Both Hodges and Earl Phillips enjoyed deep-sea fishing. One of their favorite places to fish was the Outer Banks of North Carolina and, more specifically, at Hatteras, "The Blue Marlin Capital of the World."

The two friends were such avid big-game fishermen that in 1959 they, along with friends, organized and founded the Hatteras Marlin Club. The following year they initiated the first Hatteras Blue Marlin Tournament, which quickly established itself as a signature event, drawing big-game fishermen to the waters of Hatteras. Dave's father even bought a house there.

"Every summer, my father would get me up each morning at six to get on the boat, hit the waves . . . and get seasick. My father, on the other hand, never got seasick, and he always smoked a big cigar.

"But I loved meeting the people in fishing tournaments. They have a lot of fascinating people from all over the East Coast, and I got to know them. My father was great for having me tag along."

The Hatteras Marlin Club is still thriving today. It is still best known for its Annual Invitational Blue Marlin Release Tournament held for six days each June.

While serving six years as governor, Hodges gained the reputation of attracting industry to North Carolina. That was a contributing factor that led John F. Kennedy to name Hodges secretary of commerce in 1961, the same year Dave went to Russia.

Besides the Hodges and the Phillips, also on the cruise was Gordon Gray, who served in the administrations of both President Truman and President Eisenhower. Gray, whose father was Bowman Gray, chairman of R.J. Reynolds Company, served as secretary of the army and chairman of the Presidential Foreign Intelligence Advisory Board (PFIAB). B. Everett Jordan, the North Carolina senator, was also a guest on the *Honey Fitz*.

The Hodges hosted their friends on the presidential yacht on a cruise down the Potomac River. Dave was very excited to be invited on the yacht. The *Honey Fitz* was frequently in the news as a place where President Kennedy and his wife, Jacqueline, "could escape the public eye and let their children John and Caroline run free" as they navigated the Potomac River down to Mount Vernon. They were taking the identical excursion.

They arrived at Mount Vernon late in the afternoon, just as the flag was being lowered for the day.

While the *Honey Fitz* was still anchored, with Mount Vernon in full view, the guests gathered round the table. Then Dave was approached and asked to sit at the head of the table.

Dave was surprised, and his parents were likewise puzzled at the thought of their son being in such a position. It became quickly apparent that this honor, sitting in the same chair as dignitaries from around the world, was because of his recent trip to Russia.

"They wanted me to speak because very few Americans had been to Russia at that time, and it was very unique."

I could only imagine how Dave must have felt at age nineteen, sitting at the head of this table of distinguished guests—including his parents.

Then the captain of the yacht approached Dave and said that it was customary for the person seated at the head of the table to sign the logbook of the presidential yacht. This included dignitaries such as Nikita Khrushchev, Leonid Brezhnev, Japanese Emperor Hirohito, and England's Queen Elizabeth. Dave's hands shook as he began to write his name directly under the signatures of the Shah of Iran and Haile Selassie.

"I was so nervous, I could barely sign my name," said Dave.

He spoke about his trip to Russia and his impressions of the country whose relationship with the United States wavered between strained and tenuous. Dave's trip to Russia occurred at a historic time, following the Bay of Pigs Invasion and Russian cosmonaut Yuri Gagarin becoming the first man in space, both in April of 1961. Kennedy had met with Russian premier, Nikita Khrushchev, for two days earlier that summer in Vienna. Shortly after that meeting, Khrushchev began building the notorious Berlin Wall.

Dave recalled the summer following the assassination of President Kennedy when Texas governor, John Connally, along with Hodges and Jimmy Roosevelt, the son of Franklin D. Roosevelt, were guests at the Phillips's Hatteras home for the annual Blue Marlin Release Tournament. Connally had been riding in the same car as President Kennedy and had been critically wounded by the assassin Lee Harvey Oswald on November 22, 1963. Dave remembered Connally showing his bullet wounds to the fishermen friends as he described where he was sitting in the car and how the assassination had affected him.

"He gave us an eyewitness description that I will never forget. It was just incredible.

"Here's another interesting detail," Dave added. "Years later I would be invited on the *Honey Fitz* again, and I couldn't help but ask if I could see the logbook. I was told that its whereabouts were unknown. At the time, I was also a member of the board of trustees of the Smithsonian Institute, and I discovered that the logbook had been bequeathed to the Smithsonian. But even I could not locate it."

"That is curious," I said. "What do you think happened to it?"

"I have no idea," said Dave.

# CHAPTER 7

# *Face to Face*

"So, I did finally graduate from Choate in 1961 . . . barely. Thanks to Seymour St. John."

Although the Southern boy had attended a Yankee boarding school, his father told him, "You have to come back South for college." Dave said he was both grateful and relieved at his father's pronouncement. According to Dave, at that time in the early 1960s, to North Carolinians there "was no such thing as any other college" than the University of North Carolina at Chapel Hill, often simply referred to as "Carolina."

Dave's enrollment at the school was far from automatic. Although Choate was regarded nationally as an exceptional academic institution, Dave had just barely eked by with a diploma. A college education was not a foregone conclusion.

To this day, Dave believes both his father and Seymour St. John, the headmaster at Choate, pulled some strings to get the non-academic young man accepted into Carolina. That fall, Dave pledged the Delta Kappa Epsilon (DKE) fraternity. "I was so happy to go to Carolina. I loved it. I had a great time at the DKE house," recalled Dave of his collegiate days.

While at Carolina, Dave conceded that he wasn't a very good student. "I just didn't feel good about book learning."

Yet he continued to excel in skeet shooting and competed in tournaments up and down the East Coast.

"I competed with a lot of interesting people and even shot against the marines from Camp Lejeune and the army from Fort Bragg. However, these guys would take care of me because I was a youngster. Skeet shooting helped me grow up; it was a confidence builder for me. I never had been much in school, so this is where my energy went," said Dave.

Skeet shooting remained a large part of Dave's life until his mid-twenties. In the ten years that he competed in skeet, Dave was awarded hundreds of trophies, medals, and badges in different categories, and he had been elected to the Junior All-American Skeet Team.

When Dave attended Carolina, Saturday classes were mandatory. Unfortunately, the Saturday class schedule came into direct conflict with Dave's Saturday and Sunday skeet schedule. Friday afternoons were often spent traveling to a skeet shooting location. There was no time to attend Saturday classes, so he would cut them. His academics suffered.

So, Dave left Carolina in 1965 and returned home to work at his father's textile company, Phillips-Davis Inc.

I knew Dave's father was in the American Furnishings Hall of Fame but didn't know anything about his business, so I asked him about it. Dave told me that his father had started as a salesman for DuPont, out of Virginia, selling faux leather.

"Today we all know it as vinyl," Dave explained. "It was a whole new technology for the furniture industry; not only was it cheaper than leather, it was the first washable fabric you could put on furniture."

That job led Earl Phillips to High Point, following the furniture manufacturers, and he settled there in the 1920s. In the 1930s, he started Phillips-Davis Inc., a fabric converting company, with his uncle Stanley Davis, for whom Dave is named.

In the 1950s and '60s, Phillips-Davis Inc. began to diversify into offering different products for the furniture industry. Dave's father had astutely theorized that he could sell several products to the same customer.

"'Know your customers and gain their trust, and you can sell them many products,' my dad would say. He became very successful, and he loved people."

"How did you envision your future at that time?" I asked.

"Future?" Dave responded, chuckling. "There was no such word! I was lucky just to have a job."

Dave made the most of that job, learning the textile business literally from the ground up. He began by working in the warehouse, learning about the products his father's company sold. Then Dave's father thought he needed to experience the textile industry more broadly, so he called on his friend Harry Carter, the same one who had advised him about sending Dave to Choate. As an executive at a textile manufacturing firm in New York City, Harry agreed to take Dave on as an intern in their upholstery fabric division.

By the time Dave returned to High Point about six months later, he had learned much, and his father asked him to travel nationally with the sales force.

"He told me one day, 'I know you are not a good student, but you are a good salesman. You love people like I do. Being a good student is important, but not being a good student is not going to hold you back in life. Make the most of what you have.' That always meant a lot to me.

"My father was a converter, meaning he bought fabric from large manufacturing mills and sold it by smaller amounts to furniture companies. We sent samples to buyers across America, but what we really needed to do was go to our biggest customers.

"We would go to the markets in New York, Chicago, Los Angeles, San Francisco, Dallas, and Atlanta. We did that circuit twice a year. In between those big circuits, I traveled all over America, calling on specific customers for those areas.

"Now, I was just twenty-five years old, and most of the fabric salesmen, including our competitors, were older people and, back then, mostly men. They played golf with their customers and went drinking with them. So, when it came to buying fabric, the customers were just trying to help their buddies, and here I am, trying to break in as a kid.

"I heard a lot of people say no. I probably drive my children crazy today, telling them, 'Keep knocking on doors. All you need is one door to open.' I also learned that if I wanted to succeed at sales, I needed to take time to get to know the customers."

I was impressed Dave jumped feet first into sales like that, but I felt like I was missing part of the story. "I have a question. What made you so determined and enthusiastic about your job? Was that also because of your early success with skeet shooting, or was there something more?"

Dave thought for a moment. "I think it goes back to all the things I mentioned earlier: that taste of success while skeet shooting, being comfortable with older people, and traveling with all different kinds of people to skeet tournaments through high school and college. That gave me a lot of confidence.

"But something else happened here, too. I fell in love with the fabric business.

"When I first started working for my father, I felt like a general screw-up. I was very lucky that I had a place to go. I don't think I could have gotten a regular job.

"However, in the process, I got to know the products, and I got to know the customers.

"There's something immediate about visiting customers face to face. You show them a product, and you can see immediately whether they like it or don't like it, right there on the spot. You quickly build a rapport with your customer, and you get instant feedback as to whether your product works for them or not."

"And that was something I imagine you were very good at," I said.

"I just loved it. So, it's all that: I had fun traveling America, and I love people; I'm fascinated with people. A few years later, I started traveling the world selling textiles.

"Later, I had other businesses," Dave concluded, "but none of them were as exciting as the fabric business to me."

At that, Dave and I had to stop for the day because we both had other appointments.

When we checked our calendars to schedule our next meeting, Dave discovered that he would be gone for the next couple weeks.

"Can we wait until I get back? It's very important to me that we meet face to face," Dave explained.

"People are surprised to hear that, in this day and time, I don't have an iPhone; I have a flip phone. I don't even have a computer. My assistants, Isabell and Debbie, print out my e-mails and hand them to me on paper. If I need to send a response, I'll dictate it to them, and they'll type it up and send it. Isabell even takes shorthand."

"Shorthand?" I asked.

Dave chuckled. "That's right. Isabell has been with me for twenty-eight years. I don't know what I would do without her.

"She has been absolutely steadfast; she has always been here for our family, all while raising her own—and she has three sons! How she carved out all that time for me and still took care of her family, I have no idea. She's remarkable.

"A couple years ago, she did say, 'If something happens to me, what in the world are you going to do?' So, we were lucky enough to find Debbie. The first thing we asked Debbie was whether she knew shorthand. Well, Debbie said that she did not know shorthand, and Isabell and I both said, 'You've got to know shorthand!'

"Debbie said that she was a graduate of the University of North Carolina School of Journalism, and she thought she could write as fast as Isabell could in shorthand. So, we tested her, and by golly, she could.

"Knowing Isabell was already my assistant, Debbie asked, 'What are you going to call me?'

"'What would you like to be called?' I asked.

"'Well, you said you were looking for an executive assistant.'

"'Then you are the executive assistant!' I said.

"'Well, what are you going to call me?' Isabell asked.

"'The chief of staff!' I answered. We all laughed.

"Anyway, if I'm at our home in Florida or the mountains, they'll print off my emails, put them in a box with my local newspaper, and FedEx them to me. I get two FedExes a week, which is very exciting," he chuckled.

"If it's an emergency, they'll fax me.

"So, I'm afraid I just have to do our meetings face to face and here in this office. Is that okay with you? I know I'm an old-world dinosaur," he added, chuckling. "But I think it actually helps me stay in touch with people."

I immediately agreed. I loved talking with Dave at our meetings, observing his reactions, enjoying his laughter, and seeing his eyes close as he reflected on the past, thinking of friends who had been part of his and Kay's lives and who had passed on. It was all part of the adventure.

# CHAPTER 8

# *The Heart of It All*

We continued our meetings when Dave returned. By then, we had settled into a routine: we would always begin at eleven or eleven thirty so we could have lunch brought up to us from the String & Splinter, a club and restaurant located downstairs, which also happened to have been founded by his father. That gave us the opportunity to catch up on the town's news and for Dave to give me torn scraps of paper where he had jotted one or two words, reminding him of another story he had to tell me.

Today there were two scraps of paper: one with the words "mother" and "lung cancer" and another with "Jack & Marsha" and "Kay."

First, I learned that as Dave was finding his place in the textile industry, his mother was fighting a courageous battle with lung cancer.

"She had a lot of operations and what seemed like endless radiation treatments at Duke University Hospital," he recalled. She would often say how frustrating it was that the hospital was always so dark and she had so little privacy. She died in 1970, at the age of fifty-four."

"Of course, we were devastated. I loved my mother very much, and we were very close. She was kind and always forgiving to me. It's really amazing, looking back, how nice and understanding both my parents were to me, because, as you know by now, I was a rascal.

"I never forgot how the darkness and lack of privacy bothered her as a patient. Later, Kay and I had the opportunity to fund the Lillian J. Phillips Cancer Pavilion at High Point Regional Hospital in her honor." In addition to a private entrance and a private elevator, I learned, the Cancer Pavilion was designed with skylights to allow natural light to stream into the area.

"Not long after my mother died, the local Cancer Society asked me to join their board. There I got to meet a whole different group of people than I ever would have met in business. I enjoyed learning all about my community from a whole different perspective.

"From there, one thing led to another, and I got more involved in our town. I've always felt civic involvement is very worthwhile. Well, you know," Dave said. "You're very active in High Point. It's fun!"

"It is," I agreed.

"Then one month after my mother died . . . wait. Before I tell you about that, I need to tell you about the Slanes."

Willis Slane Sr., I learned, had founded Slane Hosiery Mills, one of the most successful hosiery businesses in High Point. Willis, known affectionately as "Pops," was also a dear friend of Dave's father.

In their bachelor days, Earl and Pops often traveled together to Europe and loved to play cards. When Earl married Lil, Dave's mother, he was forty-two—nineteen years older than his bride. On their honeymoon cruise, Lil was surprised to see Pops and his wife, Meredith—who claimed they had booked a cruise on another ship and that cruise was cancelled.

"My mother swore to her dying breath that my father just wanted to have his best friend come with him on his honeymoon!" Dave laughed.

In 1954, Pops died suddenly of a heart attack. Upon the death of his best friend, Earl continued his friendship with Pops's sons, Jack and Willis Jr. And that was when Dave told me the story of the world-famous Hatteras Yachts.

"As you know, my father loved fishing, especially for marlin. He and his friends would fish the waters of Florida, the Bahamas, and the Outer Banks of North Carolina."

Hatteras, in particular, was known for its treacherous waters near Diamond Shoals, where swirling nor'easters combine with the turbulent conditions of the Gulf Stream current to create the best marlin fishing in North America.

"One day, my father and some of his friends, including Willis, went to Hatteras on one of their deep-sea fishing expeditions. Their wooden boat simply could not withstand the pounding waves and current of Diamond Shoals, where many a ship had sunk in rough waters. So, unable to do what they loved, they went back to the clubhouse of the Hatteras Marlin Club and bemoaned their fate over drinks."

Dave said that Willis had the reputation of being a character as well as an adventurer. He was an expert pilot who taught flying for the Army Air Corps in World War II and later flew "The Hump" over Burma from India to China. Willis boasted that he could build a boat that would navigate the high, turbulent waters without capsizing. This couldn't be done using wood or metal. It had to be fiberglass, which was known to be lightweight, extremely strong, less brittle, and less expensive—plus it could be easily shaped using molding processes.

Because of his great spirit of adventure (and the drinks), everyone who listened to Willis's boasting basically said, "That's just Willis talking."

"However, Willis wasn't just talking," Dave said. "One Saturday afternoon, a few months later, he came to our home with a cardboard box filled with pieces of fiberglass, articles, and drawings. I was probably about seventeen. Willis was very detailed in the specifications of the new boat, and I remember my father was very intrigued with what he had to say. It needed to be large enough for avid fishermen and their fishing gear yet luxurious enough for family cruising. Fiberglass was a newly discovered material, and many felt it might be only suited for a small runabout but not for a big boat. Willis said he would prove them wrong."

Even though Earl was skeptical about Willis's idea, he wanted to support the wishful dreamer and enticed many of his friends to invest in the young man with the big ideas. With investors, hope, and a dream, Willis took his designs to Owens-Corning Fiberglass Company and talked to noted naval architect Jack Hargrave, who deemed that this dream could come true.

The next step was to build the boat. Willis, with an intense loyalty to his hometown, announced that the boat should be built in High Point, North Carolina, to take advantage of the craftsmen nurtured by the furniture industry. According to Dave, many said, "You can't build a forty-foot yacht in High Point. That is two hundred miles from the ocean!"

But build it he did, with rented and used tools. Willis was the president of Hatteras Yachts, and Earl served as chairman. Willis rented a garage in downtown High Point that was previously a gas filling station. Among the investors, and perhaps with Willis himself, there was much apprehension as to whether the forty-foot yacht would even float. In the spring, Willis took the boat to High Point City Lake, and, to the relief of all, it floated.

Later in Morehead City, Willis's wife, Doris, and Dave's mother, Lil, both had the honor of christening the boat with champagne. Attending the christening was Luther Hodges, who invited the Phillips on the *Honey Fitz*.

In January of 1962, the Hatteras Yacht was introduced at the New York National Boat Show, extolled as the "largest plastic production-built power cruiser." Willis and his dream were not only an immediate hit but created a sensation throughout the boating world. Photos appeared in all of the New York newspapers, including the *New York Times*.

The yacht with the fiberglass hull was not the last innovation from the likable character. After Willis introduced several other models of yachts, the US Navy took notice of the innovative techniques of Hatteras.

The Vietnam War was raging in the mid-1960s. The military needed a patrol boat for the Mekong Delta. It had to be fast, highly maneuverable, small, and able to navigate the shallow, muddy waters of Vietnam. Willis, along with Hargrave, came up with the prototype design of combining a diesel jet engine with water-jet pumps. This design would remove propellers and replace them with water jets. The boat had to stop quickly, going from full speed to a complete stop within a boat's length. He built the prototype in record time for a demonstration for the navy officials.

Willis had the boat properly engineered and ready to demonstrate to the naval top brass from the Pentagon. With the brass seated in the boat, Willis, with his adventurous spirit, gave them a demonstration of a lifetime. He put the boat up to full throttle and then slammed on the brakes and put it in reverse, without so much as a hint as to the boat's velocity, to show the officers how the boat could "turn and stop on a dime" or, more accurately, within a boat's length. His ploy worked better than even Willis could have imagined. Military officers were flung around the boat, and a couple of bones were broken. Willis thought that was "funny as hell." The navy brass were not as amused, but they were impressed.

They were so impressed that the US Navy ordered two hundred and wanted them right away. Willis did not have the facilities to build two hundred boats, and there was no way Hatteras could expand that fast. The navy bought the prototypes from Hatteras and then made an agreement with a contractor on the West Coast.

"Many years later, Kay and I saw those Hatteras boats in Vietnam on the Mekong Delta," remembered Dave.

But the whole government experience apparently took a toll on Willis's health.

"Shortly after the demonstration, I got a call from my dad telling me that Willis had died of a heart attack. It was startling. The year was 1964, and he was just forty-four years old."

Hatteras Yachts would eventually capture the imagination of a defense contractor, Rockwell International, now known for the space shuttle and the B1 bomber. Hatteras continued to grow after the two companies merged.

"Willis's brother, Jack, continued to run the family business, Slane Hosiery Mills. I became very close to Jack Slane and his lovely wife, Marsha. And that leads me back to why I told you about the Slanes in the first place," Dave continued.

"Oh, that's right," I said, still in awe that Dave had personally witnessed the invention of large fiberglass boats.

"Just one month after my mother died, I attended the PGA's Greater Greensboro Open golf tournament with Jack and Marsha.

"I can tell you just where I was standing when I said to Marsha, 'Have you seen any lovely ladies lately?' Marsha told me that, the night before, she and Jack had been with a couple, Vi and Jim Anthony, and their daughter Kay. 'She is very attractive, lovely, and somebody you should call.' So, Marsha called the Anthonys, introduced me, and said that I might call, and I did.

"Our first date was to some extent embarrassing and at first seemed like anything but a rousing success. I invited Kay to a local dinner theater called Showboat. She was only nineteen at the time, seven years younger than I was. Well, the show turned out to be very boring—so boring that we left the theater.

"Now, what was I going to do? We decided to go to Cellar Anton's, a cozy Italian family-owned restaurant in Greensboro with lots of old-world ambience. We talked for hours on that first date, and it was special."

Just six months later, on Christmas night, Dave proposed to Kay on his parents' porch after their Christmas party.

"My mom and dad always had parties on Christmas night for the neighborhood. It is such a festive time, and by Christmas night, everyone is so exhausted they need a drink. Kay and I continued that tradition for many years."

They were married five months later, one year after they first met, on May 15, 1971. After their honeymoon traveling throughout Europe, Kay and Dave moved into a condominium in High Point to begin their life together.

"I think I'm very lucky that I met Kay. I've always told my girls to never, ever turn down a blind date!"

Later that evening, I thought about how easily relationships came to Dave and his family—and how creative business ideas seemed to be a natural byproduct. When Dave's father and Willis Slane were complaining together about the fishing conditions at the Hatteras Marlin Club, they had no intention of starting an innovative and lucrative boat-building business—in landlocked High Point, of all places. Yet, that's exactly what happened. I marveled at the ease with which he engaged people and how the simple delight in spending time with people was at the heart of it all.

# CHAPTER 9

# *Taking Risks*

"You had just married Kay, and you were traveling around the country as a textile salesman," I said, reviewing my notes.

"Ah, yes. During my travels, I learned that our competitors who had their own manufacturing operations were the ones continuing to grow and prosper.

"Kay's father, Jim Anthony, worked for a large textile company. In the early '70s, he told me about a weaving mill in Monroe, North Carolina, which their company owned. The mill wasn't doing well, and he said he thought the mill could be bought.

"I thought it would be a great opportunity for us to have a manufacturing base and become more competitive.

"I discussed this with Jim Foscue, who was the president of Phillips-Davis Inc. at the time, but he was not anxious to invest. He had worked with my father for his entire business life and now owned 20 percent of the company. Dad's health was declining at that time, so he had already transferred 40 percent to my brother, Phil, and 40 percent to me. Phil also didn't want to invest in the manufacturing plant, yet I was confident it was the right move for our company."

At the young age of thirty, Dave made what he said many thought was a very risky decision and personally invested his own money to buy the machinery used in the weaving mill. He then leased the building and started contract weaving, not only for Phillips-Davis Inc. but also for his competitors. He asked the employees in Monroe to stay and run the business. They agreed.

"Although a lot of people thought it was a risky idea at the time," Dave explained, "the reason I had the confidence to buy it was that they had existing management and employees. If I had to go out there and start new, I don't think I would have done it. All I had to do was just walk in the door and hope they continued to do what they had been doing.

"Also, as a salesman, I already knew a lot of people in the industry. I also knew the mill's customers included some of our competitors, which I hoped would now become our customers.

"One of those competitors, in particular, I see every now and then, and he still tells me, 'We would have never stayed in business unless you continued to sell to us, and we have always been grateful.'"

Dave's confidence paid off. "Fortunately, we soon were running three shifts with overtime on Saturday. We were very pleasantly surprised at the end of the first year when the mill made a profit," he added.

The textile manufacturing company became known as Phillips Weaving Mills and would become the largest operation of the textile company. Over the next twenty-five years, the textile company would increase its sales twenty-seven times.

"It sounds like that was a very pivotal decision," I said. "On one hand, it's amazing you had the confidence to take that risk at such a young age, but on the other, I can see how one step just led to another."

"That's right. Also, I think my mind was just structured that way, looking for opportunities. I've always been curious, especially in business."

One day, Dave told me, he got a call from one of his DKE fraternity brothers, Young Smith. Smith was developing Figure Eight Island, a small barrier island north of Wrightsville Beach in North Carolina, and he wanted Dave to consider purchasing a lot.

Figure Eight Island, named for its shape, was known for its natural beauty. It not only had vast natural vegetation but also an abundance of huge oaks, expansive sand dunes, and white sandy beaches. In addition, the location was ideal, surrounded by the Intracoastal Waterway and the Atlantic Ocean. So, Kay and Dave, along with their friends Susan and John Corpening, collaborated in building a home on Figure Eight Island. Smith had hired architect Henry Johnston to design properties to complement the natural environment of the island. In return for his architectural expertise, Johnston received one of the home lots on Figure Eight, and he designed his dream house to be built on the lot. The blueprint specified the home as a "tree house," incorporating the live oaks and nature into the design.

The Corpening and Phillips families ended up buying this natural, undeveloped lot from the architect and decided to build the tree house exactly as Johnston had designed it. The open home, built on the highest point of Figure Eight Island, featured fantastic views of the sound and was built amidst the natural landscaping of the island.

"We didn't think of it as a business investment; we did it just for the pleasure of our families—although people did think we were a little bit odd in that we didn't build on the beach. We built on the highest point on the island, up in the trees, overlooking the marsh."

Although Smith had high hopes for the development of Figure Eight Island, the recession and gas crunch in the 1970s hit Figure Eight Development Company very hard.

"The company was put into federal bankruptcy, and since we had a home there, I thought I might be able to buy the entire island at a good price. This bank was in Chicago, and I was hoping they might just want to cut their losses and get out. At the time, the island had thirty-nine homes and the potential for hundreds more. At the right price, it would be a really good investment.

"So, two lawyers and I went to federal court to negotiate for Figure Eight Island. We planned ahead of time what price we wanted, and unfortunately, we were not successful."

Continental Illinois Bank outbid Dave, and Figure Eight Island rebounded over the next few decades. Today there are 495 homes on the island. Although a bridge connects Figure Eight Island to the mainland, only residents and invited guests are allowed on the island. Such privacy for its residents and visitors has made homes on Figure Eight Island very desirable.

"Our families enjoyed our home there for about a decade, and then we sold it simply because we weren't using it as much as we wanted to," he said.

"That sounds like another good example of having the confidence to go after opportunities."

"Well, again, it wasn't whimsical. We talked ahead of time about how many lots we'd have, what roads we'd have to build, and so on. We were truly thinking about it as a developer.

"Plus, just as importantly, you have to know when to say no."

Around this time, Dave said, his father's health began to decline further.

"He really tried to take care of himself, but it was old age catching up with him. He was a great man who loved life until the end. He died in 1975, just five years after my mother. He was seventy-eight."

Dave's father's estate now needed to be divided and distributed between his two sons, including Phillips-Davis Inc., the fabric converting and sales company, and First Factors Corporation, a factoring company.

"What is a factoring company?" I asked.

"A factoring company purchases account receivables from other companies, which provides immediate credit protection for that company's operations," Dave explained.

Interestingly, I discovered, this was Dave's father's second factoring company. The first one had been Factors Inc., started by Dave's father in the late 1950s and later sold to North Carolina National Bank (now Bank of America) in the early 1970s, when operations were moved to Charlotte.

"Well, a couple of the guys who ran that company came back to High Point, and we decided to start all over again, with the same people in the same desks in the same location."

Bill Webster and Bill Crews had been president and vice president, respectively, of Factors Inc. and had the same titles in the new company; Dave's brother, Phil, returned from New York to serve as vice-president of sales. The strategy was to grow

First Factors's client base from their expertise in the home furnishing area. Phillips-Davis Inc. was their first client, as had been the case in 1957.

When Dave's father passed away, Dave's interests had already settled in textiles. So, Dave's brother, Phil, and Jimmy Foscue took First Factors, and Dave took Phillips-Davis Inc.

One of Dave's father's more unusual investments included a cemetery. He was a major investor in Guilford Memorial Park. At the time, his friends would ask him, "Why do you want a cemetery?" His answer was insightful yet amusing: "It's a great return when you can buy an acre and sell it by the plot!" In fact, Dave said, Guilford Memorial Park Board of Directors was the first board on which Dave was asked to serve when he was in his early twenties.

"I was so pleased that my dad asked me to be on the board. What I didn't realize was that there was very little business to be discussed at the meetings. When I went to the first board meeting, the only issue on the agenda was, 'How many swans are we going to buy for the lake?'"

Earl Phillips enriched his hometown in innumerable ways, well beyond his business ventures and investments. He served on the High Point City Council from 1935 to 1941 and was elected mayor of High Point in 1945.

Dave also recalled that his father had been very excited when Holt McPherson, editor of the *High Point Enterprise* and chairman of the board of trustees at High Point College (now High Point University), asked him to endow the School of Business. He said he was more than honored to do so, and today the Earl N. Phillips School of Business is an important part of High Point University.

"He also helped start the String & Splinter, as you know," added Dave.

I knew the club well. In addition to supplying our lunches during our meetings, the String & Splinter Club was High Point's premiere dining and social club. "String" referred to thread, representing the textile industry, and "Splinter" referred to wood, representing the furniture industry. Although it started as an all-male club, today it allows both men and women members.

"My dad loved playing cards with his friends; they would play almost every afternoon. He probably helped found the String & Splinter as a place to play cards with no women allowed!"

The accomplishments and contributions of Earl N. Phillips made such an impact on the furniture industry that he was inducted years later into the American Furniture Hall of Fame.

"What do you appreciate most about your father's legacy?" I asked.

Dave leaned back and closed his eyes to think a moment.

"I grew up watching my father meet and get to know people from all walks of life. He also had been mayor of High Point and very involved in our community.

"My father loved people," Dave concluded. "That's what I learned from him: to love people."

# CHAPTER 10

# *One of the Animals*

I discovered there was yet another saga intertwined into this story, one that would be pivotal not just for Dave but his entire family.

Kay had grown up in nearby Greensboro, and before she and Dave were married, she had lived for seven years on a farm outside of Greensboro called Cedar Oak Farm. Her father loved cows and horses, and Dave would soon discover that Mr. Anthony had passed his love of animals on to his daughter.

"When Kay and I were dating, I visited the Anthonys' wonderful farm with all of the animals, so I should have sensed something right then."

Kay and Dave were friends with Dr. James (Jimmy) Johnson, who was the first neurosurgeon in High Point. Johnson had been born and raised in one of the homes adjacent to this farm and had walked the land as a child.

When he returned to High Point after graduating from medical school at the University of Virginia, Johnson began to accumulate the farm's land and build his home with barns, stables, and a lake. While at UVA, he became enamored with its Georgian-style brick buildings and columns and so built his own home in the same style. He named it Shadow Valley Farm, and Dave and Kay had visited the farm several times for various functions and meetings.

"One day I was talking to Jimmy, and he said that he knew Kay and I loved his farm. Then he asked, 'Would you like to buy our farm?' I said, 'Are you talking about some acres?' He said, 'No, the house and the farm.'

"I knew Kay would love the farm because she would be able to have lots of animals."

But the purchase of the Johnson farm would not be that easy. "What we didn't know, and what would soon become a nightmare, was that Johnson had not discussed the sale with his wife and family. We were shocked and saddened about this. Now everything was up in the air. There was a time when Kay and I thought the documents were not going to be signed.

"Kay and I were to take a trip to the Bahamas with Marsha and Jack Slane. We set the departure date as a deadline to finalize the documents. The culmination was late at night when the lawyers completed final papers, and the documents were signed early in the morning.

"Kay and I arrived at the plane late, and we explained to Marsha and Jack what had occurred early that morning. In typical Jack Slane fashion, the first words out of his mouth were, 'What did you pay for it?' It drove him crazy the entire trip.

"In the end, it worked out perfectly. Looking back, it was pure fate."

After the purchase was finalized, Kay and Dave, sympathetic to the Johnson family, gave them until the end of the school year to move and then did renovations during the summer. They decided to change the name of the farm from Shadow Valley to Valleyfields.

Several years later, Kay and Dave were fortunate to purchase the adjacent Moore property that had served as a stagecoach stop in the late 1700s. That structure is now listed in the National Register of Historic Places, thanks to the help of historian Pat Plaxico.

"Pat really loved architecture and interior design and was highly regarded statewide as a historian. She's the one who educated us about the property.

"Everybody knew Pat Plaxico. She had a fabulous personality. She drove a Rolls-Royce and always wore a hat.

"Oh, that reminds me. Here's one thing that really interested me. The same architectural firm that designed my parents' home also designed Dr. Johnson's home, which is our current family home: Northup & O'Brien of Winston-Salem.

"Kay and I love living at Valleyfields Farm. Where the Johnson family once had a stable and paddocks, Kay has now filled this same area with all kinds of marvelous animals. Our family often thinks about how lucky we are; there are now twelve families who live on the property, and the farm has expanded to 405 acres. We are a real community."

While the Phillips began with the usual array of dogs, cats, ponies, and horses, it wasn't long until the farm would diversify.

Kay began by adopting "pairs" of baby animals. The first was a pair of zebras. Unfortunately, one of the baby zebras died soon after.

"It just broke Kay's heart," Dave said. Determined to find the cause, Kay implored the veterinarians from the North Carolina State College of Veterinary Medicine to conduct an autopsy on the deceased zebra. To her relief, it was found that the zebra had a congenital condition that was his doom. That zebra remains part of the Phillips's lives and is now one amongst many of the animals that have been preserved by taxidermy in the Phillips's game room.

Other animals have also included American bison. Kay presented the pair to Dave as a birthday present. Several years later, Kay gave Dave a pair of camels.

Also, during this time, as they were buying the farm and adding a menagerie of animals, the Phillips family began to grow. Kay and Dave became the parents of four daughters, and the girls loved life on the farm, riding horses, having dogs and cats, and enjoying happy childhoods.

Kay's collection of animals also became part of the family, most with personal names, such as Georgia, the zebra, and Gwenn and Gordon, the camels.

"Rosemary, the raccoon, lived in our kitchen. When she was born she was the size of your hand, and Kay fed her with an eyedropper. Kay got this little infant because a farmer had run over the nest and accidentally killed the mother raccoon. Rosemary lived in our house until she died of natural causes nine years later. She would sleep in the kitchen at night, but in the daytime, she would just scamper around the house." Rosemary, too, has been preserved by a taxidermist and lives in her favorite chair in the living room.

Morgan, the ferret, also lived in the house and went everywhere with Kay. Recently, they have added two pot-bellied pigs, Virginia and Mimi. For some time, they lived in the Phillips's kitchen, where the food was not very far away! Griffin, a terrier mix, is the newest addition to the animal entourage. Kay found her at a shelter in Florida.

"I have a funny story for you," Dave said. "It was eight thirty in the morning, and I had on my suit, ready to go to the office. The doorbell rang, and there were two North Carolina Wildlife Federation officials, wearing their Smokey Bear hats, at our door. They said, 'We have reports that you have a bear.' And I said, 'Yes, sir,' and they said that they needed to see the bear. I said, 'Okay, come on in.'

"They responded with stern faces, 'No, sir, we need to see the bear right now.' And once again I said, 'Okay, come on in.'

"So, these two men in their uniforms came on in and saw this little bear just running around. They took off their hats and got down on the floor and said, 'This is the cutest thing we have ever seen!'

"They could immediately tell that our bear was not an indigenous black bear but rather a Himalayan bear. The Himalayan bears have a white crescent on their chest. Someone had seen Kay around High Point carrying one of the bears in a papoose just like a baby with his little, furry head peeking out."

Later, following the pattern of pairs, a second Himalayan bear was added to Kay's animal entourage at Valleyfields Farm.

As a result of Kay's love and appreciation of animals of all kinds, she has been appointed to several terms on the board of directors for the North Carolina Veterinary Medical Foundation and School of Veterinary Medicine.

"This story says it all," Dave said. "One day, one of our friends from California visited our home and saw all the bears, the camels, the zebras, etc. At dinner that night, he made the comment, 'Dave, do you realize that you are just one of Kay's animals?'

"Well, when I first heard that, I was a little stunned," he confessed. "But after I thought about it, I had to admit that, yes, I am just one of Kay's animals!"

# CHAPTER 11

# *Market Square*

With the estate of his father settled and his family moved into Valleyfields Farm, Dave was able to devote more time to his business.

Attending the furniture markets in America gave Dave the perception that something more could be done within the framework of the furniture market in his hometown. It wasn't until he returned from a trip to the San Francisco furniture market that he fathomed what that could be.

"The San Francisco market was held in several old brick buildings that had been renovated as a furniture showroom complex for decorators. As I was driving to my office the next morning, I looked across the railroad tracks at the Tomlinson Furniture Company, and I thought, 'This looks just like where I was yesterday.'"

At the time, in the mid-1970s, the idea of renovating an old building would have been both venturesome and innovative. This bold idea was even riskier considering that the furniture market was still scattered throughout western North Carolina and as of yet had not completely shifted to High Point. In fact, people were worried that the furniture market might move to Dallas, Texas.

"That's when I called Bill Tomlinson, owner of Tomlinson Furniture Company, sat down with him in his office, and said, 'I have this idea of renovating your manufacturing plant into a showroom building and am wondering if you would ever work with me on that. Would you give me an option to buy your building?'"

Tomlinson thought this was a very unusual request but eventually he accepted. He agreed to an option to sell one building of 250,000 square feet at $3.00 per square foot. That would leave Tomlinson another building with 300,000 square feet, and the option could be exercised at a later date for $5.00 per square foot. The buildings were also sitting on twelve acres of land two blocks off Main Street, which was included in the deal.

Dave asked Dick Behrends, owner of the advertising firm Behrends and Associates, to be his partner. As chairman of the board of his company, Dave knew that Behrends had experience in developing and marketing real estate. They had control of the potential showroom space, but that was all it was, space. It was not even empty space—it was still being used as a furniture manufacturing plant. They agreed that Tomlinson Furniture would continue its operation, and then if the duo was successful, Tomlinson would vacate the space. Promotional material was printed. Behrends's advertising company gave it the name of Market Square.

Dave was just thirty-four years old when he purchased Market Square. "When we finally made the announcement, people thought I was crazy as hell," said Dave. "Good people. Our people!"

The idea of renovating an old building proved to be revolutionary at the time . . . too revolutionary. People wanted new buildings. They wanted dropped ceilings, carpet, and no windows. They didn't want wooden floors that creaked when walked upon. The *High Point Enterprise* wrote in October of 1976 about Market Square, "For the High Point Furniture Market, that's quite a step—some might call it audacious—but Dave and his associates have checked out all of the angles, and they said it will work."

Although it wasn't on Main Street like the other furniture showrooms, Market Square still had "accessibility to downtown and easy parking access." The partners agreed not to change the exterior of the building. They would also leave the landmark Tomlinson smokestack and water tower.

However, within a year, Tomlinson Furniture Company experienced severe financial problems. Fortunately, two investors, Jake Froelich and Chuck Haywood, bought the Tomlinson Manufacturing Operation and wanted to move into a smaller and more modern building.

"This was the best thing that could have possibly happened," Dave said. "They asked us to continue with Market Square, with the same options to purchase the buildings. Jake and Chuck had been roommates at Woodberry Forest; Chuck was in the furniture business, and Jake was in the furniture veneer business. Soon thereafter, I said, 'I think y'all should be part of this venture; as you slowly move out and we slowly move in, let's all do it together.' So, they became part of the Market Square Partnership." Two other investors who were good friends joined the group, George Lyles and Sandy Rankin.

The next semiannual High Point Furniture Market did not bring success to the new and innovative Market Square because most companies already had showroom space. The question became, how were they to attract exhibitors to Market Square?

"That's when we decided to approach companies that did not show in High Point. Thank goodness there was a company called Kittinger Furniture Company.

"Kittinger had never shown in High Point. So, I just called the president, and he said, 'We don't need to come to High Point.' I said, 'Would you please consider an offer from us?' We then offered him the original Tomlinson showroom that was already upfitted for free. He said, 'I can't turn it down. That's just too good a deal.'"

Kittinger Furniture Company became the first tenant in Market Square.

"They were really our stamp of approval in the industry and gave us credibility. We gave them showroom space, and within two years, the first phase of 250,000 square feet was full of tenants. We were very fortunate."

The growing popularity of the new Market Square showrooms necessitated the Market Square Partners to exercise the "option to buy" on the remaining part of the building. Up until then, Tomlinson Furniture Company had continued manufacturing in the 300,000 square feet in the original building.

"It was during this time that Haywood and Froelich considered selling Tomlinson Furniture Company. I contacted Jim Becher, president of the Geneva

Corporation, an investment company in Greensboro. I had never met Jim, but I knew Geneva owned a furniture company in Pinehurst, North Carolina, so I asked him if he would consider buying Tomlinson. After many meetings with Jake and Chuck, they reached an agreement. We were then able to exercise our second option for the remaining 300,000 square feet so we could complete Market Square and focus on finding tenants.

"One tenant, Natuzzi Italia of Copenhagen, Denmark, was the largest leather furniture manufacturer in the world. Pasquale Natuzzi was phenomenal, and he had great flair, but he had never been to an American market."

Natuzzi soon recognized the value of High Point for his company. He came to Market Square and created a dramatic space using the two large floors he rented for his ultra-modern leather sofas.

Natuzzi would experience much success in High Point at Market Square. That was the good news for the Market Square Partnership. The bad news was he became so successful that Natuzzi decided to establish his own building next door. That building was futuristically designed in the shape of a ship by the architect Mario Bellini and has since become an attraction in the Furniture Market area.

The showrooms filled, and the name of Market Square became much more than an asterisk in the International Home Furnishings Market. Kittinger was the spark that got Market Square going, but it was Buck Shuford of Century Furniture that laid the foundation by leasing 45,000 square feet. Market Square became "the place to be."

"In 1977, at 550,000 square feet, it was the fifth largest national historic preservation project in America," said Dave.

Market Square was founded as a traditional furniture showroom complex with long-term leases for exhibitors, where the industry standard was five years. Yet the Market Square Partnership discovered an opportunity with their newly acquired showroom space.

"Prospective tenants said, 'We don't want to sign a lease for five years. We would like to come to High Point and show our wares and see if we will be successful. We would like a temporary space and are willing to pay a higher rent to give us an opportunity with flexibility,'" he said.

The Market Square Partnership considered this experimental idea and decided to take the basement of Market Square and lease it on a "temporary" basis. Temporary partitions were erected, curtains were hung . . . whatever configuration anyone needed.

Market Square pioneered the innovative concept of temporary showroom space, and it proved to be highly successful. Suddenly, the word was out that if you came to High Point for the first time, you could show your product on a market-to-market basis without signing a big-money lease. The word spread like wildfire, and Market Square's temporary suites became the hottest concept around. It quickly spread to the rest of the High Point showroom complexes.

This seemingly simple theory has added immensely to the flexibility of the High Point Furniture Market. The temporary spaces continue to bring life to the market and have become incubators for permanent leases. This "temporary" idea has become a permanent fixture.

The history of Market Square was the primary reason I wanted to talk to Dave in the first place, and I found its history fascinating.

"I may be getting ahead of the story, but how big is Market Square now?" I asked.

"It's now about 2,250,000 square feet—approximately the same size as the office space in the Empire State Building," said Dave.

"Wow," I said, surprised.

"Believe it or not, if you put all the showroom buildings in downtown High Point together, you'd have five Empire State buildings.

"There's still plenty of opportunity today."

# CHAPTER 12

# *An Investor in People*

Once again, Dave's father-in-law, Jim Anthony, had a keen eye for a good business deal, and this time it was a hosiery mill.

"Kay's father had told me about a new hosiery mill in Hickory, North Carolina, that was the most updated mill since World War II. He said, 'Everything is the very best at Pons Hosiery, but they are in bankruptcy. Why don't you buy it and have some of your friends in High Point run it, since you don't know a thing about hosiery?'"

Dave was interested but also heeded the advice of his father-in-law. "I made a bid to buy it out of US Bankruptcy Court in Richmond, Virginia, and asked a friend, Don Lindner, the president of the largest hosiery company in High Point, to run it and be an investor. He agreed."

Unfortunately, their offer wasn't accepted—which was when Lindner suggested they buy another hosiery mill: Annadeen Hosiery Mill in Burlington, North Carolina.

Lindner and Dave put together a deal to purchase the mill and went to Bob Niebauer of First Union Bank to finance the purchase. This was not Niebauer and Dave's first business transaction; Niebauer helped to finance First Factors in the early 1970s. Plus, First Union had just opened a new office in High Point, so the timing was perfect to approach them for financing. Niebauer created the financial package with First Union City executive Dick Meadows, who also happened to be Kay's distant relative.

Then, just six months after First Factors had been distributed to Dave's brother, Phil, and Jimmy Foscue through the settlement of their father's estate, Dave received a call from Dick Meadows and Bob Niebauer.

"They wanted to start a savings and loan company," Dave explained. "There was a new federal law that encouraged the transfer from a savings and loan depository ownership to a shareholder ownership. However, after much discussion, I recommended we start another factoring company."

Meadows and Niebauer agreed and joined with Dave to start Phillips Factors.

To establish the new factoring company, they had to work with a different bank than First Union because Meadows and Niebauer did not want a conflict of interest.

"We also could not go to North Carolina National Bank [now Bank of America]," added Dave, "since the original Factors Inc. had been sold to them several years before. Wachovia became the obvious choice. We were also fortunate to learn about two banks from eastern North Carolina that were moving to the area: Southern National Bank and BB&T.

"We used our textile company as a base of business and proceeded to enter the factoring business a third time. Would you believe that we started in the same office with the same desks all over again?" Meadows and Niebauer would eventually manage and build Phillips Factors.

As Phillips Factors evolved in the late 1970s, another offshoot company called Phillips Financial was formed. Phillips Financial was a unique company in that it financed temporary personnel agencies. In those days, the demand for temporary workers was high, and small "mom and pop" agencies were located all across America.

"Often these agencies lived the 'hand-to-mouth' type of financial lifestyle. They had to pay their personnel every week but would only receive payment from the clientele companies once a month. These agencies did not have the capital funds on hand to pay the people who worked on a weekly basis, so they would approach our factoring business," said Dave. Phillips Financial expanded nationwide and became one of the largest temporary finance companies in the country.

During the same time, in the late seventies, the Phillips Textile Group was formed, which included a knitting mill, velvet mill, weaving mill, printing mill, and a mill in Canada. Along with Phillips Factors, Phillips Financial, and Phillips International (which managed textile sales outside America), these corporations were consolidated under the name of Phillips Industries.

The purchase of Phillips Mills of Canada posed a new challenge to Dave, a challenge that had nothing to do with negotiations, manufacturing, or business operations. This challenge was one of communiqué. Phillips bought an existing Canadian textile mill to expand the customer base by selling to Canadians. The plant was located in Montreal, Quebec.

Dave chuckled as he reminisced about the diversity of the Quebec plant. "It was the most fun and the most interesting. We had a financial officer named Henry Wong, who was Chinese but spoke French. He used an abacus to do costing. Wong would bang the balls along the steel rod. I would say, 'Henry, let's do it on the calculator. We're going to lose our shirts.' He would knock those balls around and make us so nervous. Larry Lewis, our corporate financial officer, would use his calculator, and much to our amazement, Henry was always right. We were just dumbfounded."

The sales manager was Dave Diamond and the plant manager was Maurice Payment, and both spoke French. Neither Dave nor Lewis spoke French. Dave added lightheartedly, "Since Larry and I didn't speak French, by Quebec law we were supposedly not allowed to communicate with the employees.

"I've spent a lot of time in Montreal. We love it." He sat forward in his chair. "Go to Montreal," he said to me directly. "It's beautiful. Everybody speaks French, and it has great restaurants."

"Okay, I will," I said, smiling.

Through my research, I knew that Dave had often said he appreciated his associates and surrounded himself with quality people. That was evidenced by a statement he made in March of 1988 in an interview with *North Carolina Magazine*: "One thing I tell our people who are managing the businesses is that

I want them to enjoy themselves; their families and their lives come first. If they are not happy at home or happy in their lives, they're not going to be very happy in their work."

"I've read that you really invested in your managers and you wanted to make sure they were happy at home and at work," I said to Dave. "Can you tell me more about your principles or philosophies behind a successful business?"

"Here's a philosophy I've had from the beginning," he replied. "Back when I diversified into manufacturing, I didn't know a thing about manufacturing. So, I tried to find the best person to run each operation.

"But here's another important part of that philosophy: at each corporation, I decided to let the management worry about the profits.

"I wanted to hire the best people to run these different organizations with the mindset of an owner. An owner is very different than a manager. The sales force would get a commission, of course, but the people who ran sales would negotiate pricing with the people in manufacturing. The manufacturers had an incentive to build in profit, while sales had an incentive to market the product. Together, they could usually figure out the best situation for each company.

"Another thing you might find interesting is that I was, to my knowledge, the first person to hire a female plant manager in our industry. It was in our knitting mill in Rutherford, North Carolina, and this lady was terrific. She was a basketball coach for her town's high school, just a true leader. Sadly, she was later killed in a car wreck.

"I was also one of the first in our industry to hire female salespeople to travel on the road. At that time, it was usually the men who would travel: they would go out, drive to different states, check into a motel, visit different customers and take them out to dinner, and drive to the next place on the next day.

"But two ladies came to me individually and said they would like to have their own sales territory. I'll never forget; one of them said, 'I understand that salesmen make a lot of money. Well, I would like to make a lot of money.' I discussed it with our sales manager and our sales team, and we said, let's give it a try.

"Both ladies were really, really good. Unlike the men, who wanted to talk about golf or baseball, or have a beer afterwards, they'd always ask for the order, get on the road, and go to the next customer."

Then Dave told me about an unusual business opportunity completely unrelated to the textile business.

"One day, I received a call from Earl Slick, who asked me out of the blue, 'Would you be interested in investing in a plane with me?'"

Dave explained that he had met Slick earlier, when Slick had been in the process of converting Brookstown Mill, an old cotton mill in Winston-Salem that was recognized as the community's oldest factory, into a bed and breakfast with various shops and a restaurant. The mill complex had been listed on the National Register of Historic Places, so the conversion had to be a restoration rather than a renovation. Slick was aware that Dave had restored the Market Square Complex, so at the time he had sought his advice on the restoration.

Among his many other business ventures, Slick owned the full-service aviation company Atlantic Aero, based at Piedmont Triad Airport in Greensboro, North Carolina. In addition to owning planes, Slick leased them and had the facilities and the crew to maintain them. In North Carolina, his business ventures were much more comprehensive than his aviation interests, yet his love remained in aviation.

Slick had also learned of Dave's interest in aviation. Unbeknownst to Dave, Slick had been interested in expanding his aviation operation into a jet chartering service. And that's what gave rise to the unexpected phone call.

Dave knew he had been given an opportunity that he could not refuse. That call led to the duo owning different planes over a period of twenty-five years. It was also the beginning of a deep, lifelong friendship. Dave knew that Slick had come from a very interesting family, but the extent of Slick's colorful history he found truly fascinating.

Apparently, Slick came from a family that had garnered international headlines since the days when his father, Thomas Slick, had been known as the "King of the Wildcatters." In addition to the publicity received by his father, both Slick's uncle and brother gained international media attention.

Dave had always known that Slick was somewhat protective of his persona. In spite of his very visible business dealings, Slick chose to keep a modest and low profile in his adopted town of Winston-Salem.

Years later, Dave would learn that his demeanor was due to a very public crime and trial concerning the kidnapping of his uncle. His uncle, Charles F. Urschel, became the center of one of the most notorious kidnappings in the 1930s. His kidnapping by the Machine Gun Kelly gang and the kidnapping of the son of Charles Lindbergh were the most publicized kidnappings at the time and changed federal and state laws forever.

It was that kidnapping that would forever be etched in the psyche of Earl Slick, even as he moved from Texas to North Carolina. His wealth was no secret, and he expressed concerns to his friends of his own possible kidnapping. Slick was also a renowned animal art collector and quietly displayed his valuable art collection in his office in the basement of the Thruway Shopping Center, which he had developed.

"It was said that Slick was so publicity-shy that when asked what his profession was, he would often reply, 'I am a dog trainer,'" Dave said, laughing.

"Every few years, Slick would call me and say, 'Partner, we have just made a deal on another plane.' Slick loved to speculate on airplanes."

One of those planes was the Citation X, still known as the fastest civilian aircraft in the sky. Its cruising speed is just shy of the sound barrier at Mach 0.92 (700 miles an hour). Slick was excited when he called Dave with the news: "I was just able to make a great deal on a new plane, partner." Upon listening to Slick's engaging description of their purchase, Dave couldn't help but get excited as well.

"I was just happy to invest with him."

The aerodynamics of this new Citation X met all their expectations and even exceeded them, and therein lay the trouble. The Citation X was undoubtedly an incredible plane, but because it was so fast, on certain runways that asset became a liability. The Citation could not land on shorter runways.

This made the Citation impractical for chartering, so they merged with NetJets, owned by Warren Buffett, a company that offers fractional ownership and rental of private business jets.

"Very interesting," I said. I could see a consistent theme emerging.

"It sounds like the common denominator to all your business investments is trust in the people you're working with, isn't it? I can see how knowing people well and meeting with them face to face allows you to trust them, which allows you to further invest in them—whether by making them owner/managers or investing money in their ideas—which creates better results."

"Exactly," Dave said.

"When it comes down to it, I am just an investor, and I invest in people."

# CHAPTER 13

# Bush Comes to High Point

As Phillips Industries was thriving and his children growing, Dave was asked to help raise money for Ronald Reagan, who was seeking his first term as president of the United States.

"I had seen Ronald Reagan speak at a major rally at the Greensboro Coliseum, and after the rally, I got a call from Paul Sticht, who was president of R.J. Reynolds Tobacco Company at the time. He asked me, 'Would you help me gather some donors from High Point? We're having Ronald Reagan at a luncheon in several weeks,' and I was honored to do so."

They hosted their fundraiser luncheon at Graylyn Estate, the home of Bowman Gray, former president and chairman of R.J. Reynolds Tobacco Company, in Winston-Salem.

"I don't know if you've ever been, but it's magnificent. Graylyn was designed in 1929 by Luther Lashmir, the same architect who designed my parents' home and who also designed our home in Roaring Gap, which I'll tell you about later. And his company designed our Valleyfields home. Isn't that amazing?"

"Yes, it is. That architect is the thread through your whole life, isn't he?"

Dave said Graylyn also provided a very intimate atmosphere where people could stand and talk to Reagan.

"It was just an incredible experience to witness the wonderful outpouring of support for Reagan. He was charming, as you can imagine, and he wore one of his signature brown suits. Everybody loved him, and we raised a lot of money."

The fundraiser was so successful that Kay and Dave were later invited to the presidential inauguration and the Inaugural Ball in 1981. I was amazed to find out they stood just a few feet from where the iconic photo of Nancy Reagan was taken (known as the "Nancy photo"), in which she was dressed in her beaded, one-shouldered white sheath Galanos gown, dancing at the ball. They also attended the swearing-in ceremony, and according to Dave, "It was just one of those unforgettable moments in your life. Reagan changed the nation and changed the world."

Dave said it was that Ronald Reagan campaign and the excitement of being part of the political process that inspired his enthusiasm for politics. "From that moment on, I got more involved."

One of Ronald Reagan's biggest supporters was Senator Helms of North Carolina. Helms was such an ardent Reagan supporter that he had been suggested as a potential running mate for Reagan in his 1980 presidential bid; however, it was George H.W. Bush who became the vice-presidential candidate.

In the political arena, Helms proved to be a very colorful figure. "Helms was this larger-than-life figure who was playing an enormous role in politics, controversial to some and meaningful to others. He dealt with issues in a straightforward way."

Several years later, Helms asked Dave to host a fundraiser for him at Valleyfields Farm. Howard Baker, chief of staff to President Reagan and former Senate majority leader, came to Valleyfields and helped to organize the Helms fundraiser.

Helms was running once again for a US Senate seat, and his opposition would be Governor Jim Hunt, who had served as the governor of North Carolina for eight years. He had then decided to run for the North Carolina US Senate seat.

The race for the Senate seat was not only the most expensive in US history at the time, it was also very, very intense. Helms won the 1984 election, and Hunt temporarily retired from politics and joined a prominent law firm but would be reelected governor again eight years later. He would become the only North Carolina governor who served four terms.

Hunt would also not forget Dave Phillips, as I would later discover.

As the Phillips's daughters were getting older, Kay's interests in the cultural arts began to flourish. Kay was also developing a close relationship with Nancy Lyles and Mazie Froelich, the wives of two of her husband's Market Square partners. Although there was a vast difference in the ages of the three women, they formed a deep and everlasting friendship. As the youngest of the trio, Kay looked to and admired the community and cultural commitments of her two friends.

"Kay was raising our girls and was intimately involved in our community and our state of North Carolina. She was asked to join several state-level boards for organizations such as the North Carolina Museum of History, the North Carolina Museum of Art, the North Carolina Arts Council, the North Carolina Dance Theatre, the North Carolina Symphony, and the North Carolina State University College of Veterinary Medicine, among others.

"During that time, Kay traveled the state far more than I did and knew so many people in North Carolina. When I got into state government a decade later, Kay already knew all of these people. Everybody really admired her dedication and leadership."

One day, in 1985, Kay and Dave received a phone call requesting that they host Vice President Bush at their home. Their answer was an enthusiastic yes.

Dave, having been vice-chairman of the board of directors of the High Point Hospital, posed a special request to the vice president's campaign team. High Point was having a groundbreaking for its new hospital, High Point Regional Health System, on November 8, 1985. Would the vice president preside at the ceremony for the new facility? He accepted, and Bush congratulated High Point on the construction of its new hospital and, more importantly, on "the propensity of one American to help another."

Bush's visit to High Point also included a reception at Market Square followed by a private reception at the Phillips's Valleyfields Farm. Excitement began to build as soon as the US Secret Service sent an Advance Team to High

Point to check out the security provisions, the routes, and all of the venues of the visiting vice president. The Advance Team landed their cargo jet at the Piedmont Triad Airport. The jet was equipped with everything, including the limousine that would transport Bush. The roads at Valleyfields Farm were not the most conducive for limousine travel.

At first, the Secret Service drove the bulletproof limousine in through the front entrance of the farm on Shadow Valley Road. They drove, or attempted to drive, around the farm's lake to get to the Phillips's home. They had not anticipated the dirt roads that, should it rain, could easily turn into a solitary quagmire, potentially entrapping the vice president in his own limousine. The bulletproofing of the vice-presidential car substantially added to the burdensome weight of the limousine. Therefore, becoming embedded in the mud was a remote possibility that the Secret Service did not wish to become a reality.

There had to be an alternate route into Valleyfields Farm that would not impede the motorcade. The back entrance to the farm resolved the dilemma and was able to accommodate the twenty-two-car motorcade, which included an ambulance and back-up cars.

The itinerary for the motorcade was not the only security measure taken on the Phillips's farm. The Secret Service Advance Team remained on the farm for an entire week before Vice President Bush arrived in High Point for a one-day visit. They set up an office on the farm, and the Secret Service scanned the entire area of the farm twenty-four hours a day.

The day of Bush's visit finally arrived. Before greeting the invited guests downstairs in the Phillips's home, Bush came through the back door and spent time upstairs with the Phillips family. He had flown in from Texas that day and immediately requested a drink. He was friendly and relaxed as he descended the stairway to meet the friends of the Phillips.

"It was very exciting and a great honor to introduce the next president of the United States," Dave said.

Bush entered the game room and didn't say a word but just looked around, gazing particularly at the taxidermied, antlered animals on the wall.

"I had shot these animals while on a safari in Africa thirteen years earlier. They all had very large horns, and Bush just looked at the crowd and said, 'Those horned animals remind me of my four horny sons.'"

Eighteen years later, when son George W. was the forty-third president of the United States, the Phillips were seated at the head table next to him at a fundraising luncheon in Raleigh.

"There were a lot of people at the luncheon," Dave said, "and it was a very exciting time. I mean, what do you talk to the president about? So, I said, 'Mr. President, may we tell you about your dad coming to our home and what he said?'

"He perked up and said, 'Tell me about it. My mom and dad tell the worst stories about the family.' I said, 'Well, sir, this is a story about you and your brothers,' and he said, 'Tell me.' I told him the story of the four horny sons. He reared back laughing as the audience wondered what in the world we were talking about!"

Then the president turned the tables on the Phillips and said to them, "Let me tell you one." He told the Phillips about the time when the Bush housekeeper in Texas came to his mother and told her that she was very worried because something peculiar had happened. She said that the laundry reeked with a terrible odor and nothing she did could get rid of it. Barbara Bush smelled the odor and decided it smelled just like urine. Suspecting her rambunctious sons, she called her four sons together and demanded they tell her what was going on.

Nobody would say anything until one of the brothers sheepishly raised his hand and confessed that he was to blame. He had "whizzed" in the steam iron! Quite surreptitiously and notably, the forty-third president of the United States did not tell Dave who the "offender" was in this mischievous caper. However, recently, Kay and Dave were with Jeb Bush, who knew the story well. He told them who it was, but Dave said, "We have decided to keep it confidential."

# CHAPTER 14

# The Movie Studio

The friendship between Dave and Kay Phillips, Jake and Mazie Froelich, and George and Nancy Lyles continued to thrive. The three partners traveled to furniture markets in Europe and the Far East endeavoring to persuade companies to come to High Point and, more specifically, to Market Square to showcase their products at what had become the largest furniture market in the world—the International Home Furnishings Market. With their wives, the Market Square partners also traveled extensively and became close friends.

What I found so remarkable about the partnership and subsequent friendship was that the trio represented three different generations.

George Lyles was the older statesman. "He was a pure Southern gentleman. George always wore a coat and a tie; he was very old school. He was a lovely man and just a pleasure to have as a partner. The Lyles were fabulous and dear people whom we loved."

Age-wise, between the Lyles and the Phillips were the Froelichs. According to Dave, Jake Froelich was a dynamic personality who had a new idea every minute. Mazie and Jake eventually moved into the penthouse "above the store" of Market Square and were involved with Market Square every day of their lives.

"Well, one day Froelich came up with one of his novel ideas to present to Lyles and me. He proposed that a movie sound stage studio be built in High Point!"

At first, Dave said, they were very skeptical at the thought. Then, as Froelich explained his idea further, he became more and more convincing. Eventually, the idea of building a film studio in High Point did not seem so unrealistic after all.

"We figured that the movie industry was a growth industry, not only for High Point but for all of North Carolina," Dave explained.

In my research, I discovered Dave spoke about the studio and film production in a 1988 interview with *North Carolina Magazine:*

> Carolina Atlantic Studios is an outgrowth of an idea that Jake Froelich and Sid Gayle had during the filming of a Richard Pryor movie here in High Point in 1985. *Critical Condition* was not acclaimed as one of the better pictures artistically, but still it was profitable. The thing that intrigued us is that the people who made *Critical Condition* appreciated the tremendous savings that they were able to achieve in High Point. We at Market Square built sets for them . . . sets that they claimed were better than what they could get in Hollywood or New York at a much more reasonable price. Just the overhead in High Point, such as room and board, was obviously much better, and the local technical people they could draw upon was outstanding. Therefore, the number of people they had to bring in from New York or California would be greatly reduced, and they would be able to put together a film for less. For example, the producers of *Critical Condition* claimed they saved half of the cost by making the film in North Carolina. We have been told that once we get up and running, that there is absolutely no reason other people won't come in here and use these facilities, and

not just to make full-length motion pictures. You can make TV programs, all kinds of ads, videos, etc.

In addition, world-renowned film producer Dino De Laurentiis formed the De Laurentiis Entertainment Group and built a studio complex (now EUE/Screen Gems) in Wilmington, North Carolina. He chose North Carolina as the location for his DEG Studios after filming Stephen King's *Firestarter* on the nearby Orton Plantation. De Laurentiis considered North Carolina an ideal place to set up his studio because of the state's diverse topography from mountains to beaches. This gave rise to North Carolina becoming one of the most popular locations for filmmaking in the eastern United States.

As an added attraction, in 1980 Governor Hunt had established the North Carolina Film Office to create new jobs while promoting the state of North Carolina. North Carolina School of the Arts in neighboring Winston-Salem established a film school so there would be an abundance of qualified film technicians.

A film studio in High Point—yes, it could be successful, or so the partners thought.

So, they built a state-of-the-art sound stage, Carolina Atlantic Studios, big enough to build many movie sets and equipped with an editing room, a theater to screen dailies, and even an underground swimming pool that could be used to film underwater sequences.

Froelich's proposition did not end with a film studio. They would need a place for the film offices and overnight accommodations for actors and crew. His vision of what a film studio could mean to High Point was idyllic, and his optimism and enthusiasm persuaded the partners that perhaps Froelich did have a groundbreaking idea.

Carolina Atlantic Studios was soon built, and the Market Square Partnership also bought the adjacent 104-room Howard Johnson Motel. They then invested in Alderman Studios, a commercial photography studio that served the furniture industry, which at the time was the largest still photography studio in America, so it was an ideal partner for layout and set design for movies.

The inaugural effort for the Carolina Atlantic Studios was to be a feature film, *The First Year*, co-produced by John Daly's Hemdale Film Corporation (*Platoon* and *The Last Emperor)* and Martin Poll (*The Lion in Winter*). Although that film never made it to fruition, many films were produced through the High Point studio. Among them was *House of Cards* starring Tommy Lee Jones and Kathleen Turner.

The Carolina Atlantic Studios eventually became one of two studio locations for the Market Square Partners. Froelich purchased Highland Cotton Mill, a vacant yarn manufacturing plant located south of Market Square on Mill Avenue, at a bankruptcy auction in 1996. Dave remembers the incident vividly.

"My family and I were staying at the famous Giraffe Manor in Nairobi, Kenya. They have the largest collection of reticulated giraffe in the world. We would be eating breakfast, and they would stick their heads through the window. I was surprised when my assistant Isabell faxed me an article from the *High Point Enterprise*. The headline read, 'Market Square Partners Purchase Highland Yarn Mills.'"

Years after the investment, unfortunately, it became obvious that the dream of a thriving film studio in High Point was just not going to work. Lyles and Dave decided the best thing to do was to donate the film sound stage to the North Carolina School of the Arts so they could use it to train their students in filmmaking.

The next step was to persuade Froelich to agree. Both Lyles and Dave realized that this ultimate resolution would mean the end to Froelich's dream. Although Froelich was saddened, he acknowledged the wisdom of the financial decision and signed the papers, albeit reluctantly.

Although many people might look at the building of a film studio as a failed venture, Dave looked at it as an adventure, a great experience. His continual optimism led to a gift from Kay, a red leather placard with gold embossing inscribed with *No Whining,* which still occupies a prominent place on his desk in his Market Square office. There was "no whining" when Carolina Atlantic Studios fell flat. At a time when others may be overwhelmed or disappointed, Dave looked at it as an interesting opportunity.

To his family and many of his friends, he is an "incurable optimist." I shared with him an article I found in the 1988 *Triad Business Magazine*, where he commented,

> I really do look at the world as just an opportunity. Sometimes I get frustrated that I can't experience so much. I feel very fortunate to have been born in High Point, mainly because it is on the verge of really being an integral part of a dynamic area. It's all going to be wonderful for everyone!

"Really, I just love to get involved," Dave said. "I walk into a gathering, and I want to meet everybody in the room. I especially love to meet new people and ask them where they're from and what they do."

Dave sat quietly for a moment. "It is amazing that George and Nancy and Jake and Mazie are no longer with us. They were all a very important part of our lives, and we loved them dearly."

# CHAPTER 15

# The Market Square Tower

S oon Market Square required further expansion. "One day, our largest exhibitor, Century Furniture Company, said they needed more space. So, we decided to add a tower adjacent to the existing building."

As they were considering an architect for the tower, Dave remembered the Odell family.

The Odell family had been in the textile business for generations, since 1877, and they owned Randolph Mills Textile Company in Concord, North Carolina, one of the suppliers to the Phillips Textile Group. Arthur Gould "Gouley" Odell Jr. also happened to be a famous commercial architect. Dave had been impressed by the buildings designed by Odell in downtown Charlotte, and eventually his company, A.G. Odell Associates, was retained as the architectural firm for Market Square Tower.

The resulting Market Square Tower became the first mixed-use building in the state of North Carolina, harmoniously combining condominiums over an office complex and showrooms in one building. Odell's design was very avant-garde at the time for North Carolina—so avant-garde that no building codes existed to govern the mixed-use building.

According to Dave, "We had to go to the state and change the laws to accommodate the tower. Interestingly, under the new codes, we were allowed to have a swimming pool on the fifteenth floor!"

The first five floors were an extension of the original building's showroom space. The next six floors were offices. The top floors consisted of nineteen condominiums. In addition, there was another added amenity, underground parking with twenty-four-hour security.

Now Market Square had more than enough room to expand. "I had already moved our fabric offices to the Tower, but then I thought, *We've got to fill all this space up. Let me see if our textile competitors would also like to move their offices here, instead of being scattered all over High Point.*" Dave's appeal was met positively, and soon Market Square Tower was filled with textile companies, even his best competitors. The tower became known as the Textile Tower.

To complement the diverse architecture of old and new, the partners called upon Pat Plaxico, renowned designer and decorator, for the interior design of Market Square. Pat had been the historian who had helped Dave and Kay receive the historical designation for the stagecoach stop on their property.

"Pat is the genius who created the charm and atmosphere of the Market Square Complex. She not only laid out the sites for the showrooms, but she also designed an atmosphere of openness with storefronts with large glass windows. It was just remarkable to see her work."

Additionally, the Market Square Partnership thought that the currently vacant Tomlinson executive offices in Market Square would be an ideal new location for the String & Splinter Club. Plaxico did the design renderings to be presented to the String & Splinter Board of Directors as well.

However, there was a major hurdle in convincing the String & Splinter to move to the Market Square Complex. They didn't have the money to move. However, this would not deter the partners in accomplishing their goal, and they made the club a proposal: The Market Square Partners would agree to pay for the renovations to accommodate the club and charge them the same rent. If the String & Splinter did not get any new members, then they would not have to pay the Partnership back for the move; however, if their membership grew, then the club could pay the Partnership back. Both agreed to this proposal, and the String & Splinter and Market Square both prospered by the move.

Today, the String & Splinter continues to thrive while many of the private clubs in surrounding cities have not fared as well. Dave said, "The String & Splinter is a welcoming place. Barbara Garry, who retired after thirty-one years at the String & Splinter, started as the social director before becoming general manager; she did a fabulous job. People loved her and her staff. As the String & Splinter enters a new phase, the club remains very important to our community: socially, civically, and business-wise."

Now that the textile companies had become more centralized at Textile Tower, Dave and some of the other textile exhibitors had an idea.

"Instead of traveling to our customers all over America," said Dave, "why don't we have a show in High Point where our customers already have showrooms?" The textile industry understood the opportunity as did the furniture companies. So, the industry created an organization called the International Textile Manufacturers Association (ITMA) and a textile show called Showtime™.

Today, Showtime is a semi-annual fabric market that brings all segments of the home furnishings industry together, in one place and at one time. It is internationally acclaimed; several thousand people attend Showtime twice a year. They also have special events, seminars, and forums. It brings the world to the home furnishings capital of the world.

The Market Square Textile Tower now features more than eighty fabric manufacturers on five floors. At the time, Phillips Industries became the largest rental tenant in the Market Square Complex. The Phillips Textile executive offices and showrooms were located on two different floors, while Phillips Factors and Phillips Financial were located on another floor.

Later, I was thinking about how some of Dave's investments succeeded while others did not—yet he approached every new opportunity with the same enthusiasm.

I remembered a saying entitled *Attitude* by Charles Swindoll that I had seen in his office:

*The longer I live, the more I realize the impact of attitude on life. Attitude, to me, is more important than the past, than education, than money, than circumstances, than failures, than successes, than what other people think or say or do. It is more important than appearance, giftedness, or skill. It will make or break a company . . . a church . . . a home. The remarkable thing is that we have a choice every day regarding the attitude we will embrace for that day. We cannot change the fact that people will act in a certain way. We cannot change the inevitable. The only thing we can do is play on the one string we have, and that is our attitude . . .*

*I am convinced that life is 10% what happens to me and 90% how I react to it. And so it is with you . . . We are in charge of our attitudes.*

That seemed to sum up Dave Phillips's attitude perfectly.

# PHOTO SECTION

Dave shooting at the High Point Skeet Club with Horace G. Ilderton
with his six-inch shoe before his leg amputation.
Photo Credit: Phillips Family Archives.

Dave skeet shooting while sitting on a stool at the Roaring Gap Club in the mountains of North Carolina two months after the amputation of his lower leg. Photo Credit: Phillips Family Archives.

Market Square Complex had expanded to 1,050,000 square feet, while retaining the original water tower and smokestack, when sold to Vornado Realty Trust in 1998. Photo Credit: Fred Blackman.

*To Kay and Dave Phillips With best wishes,* Ronald Reagan

President Reagan welcomes Kay and Dave Phillips to the White House. Photo Credit: Courtesy of US State Department.

US Senator Helms and his "remarkable friend" Dave Phillips meeting in Helms's office in Washington, DC. Photo Credit: US Congressional Office.

Vice President Bush pointing to African animal heads on the wall while
visiting Kay and Dave Phillips in their home at Valleyfields Farm.
Photo Credit: Phillips Family Archives.

President Bush welcomes Dave Phillips to the White House.
Photo Credit: US State Department.

Jake and Mazie Froelich, Kay and Dave Phillips, and Nancy and George
Lyles at the groundbreaking for the Carolina Atlantic Movie Studio.
Photo Credit: Phillips Family Archives.

Dave Phillips, board member of the North Carolina Department of
Transportation, speaking at the groundbreaking for the
US 311/US 74 Bypass around High Point.
Photo Credit: North Carolina Department of Transportation.

Kay with Himalayan bear named Jane that she raised from a baby cub.
Photo Credit: Phillips Family Archives.

North Carolina Governor Jim Hunt in Secretary Phillips's office
at the Department of Commerce in Raleigh.
Photo Credit: North Carolina State Department.

The lighting and passing of the Flame of Hope at the Sacred Site of Pnyx near
the Temple of Olympus in Athens, Greece, for the Special Olympics World
Games in North Carolina. Photo Credit: Special Olympics World Games.

Stevie Wonder performs at the opening ceremony for the
1999 Special Olympics World Games in Raleigh, North Carolina.
Photo Credit: Special Olympics of North Carolina.

Kay holding Rosemary, the raccoon that she rescued as a baby.
Photo Credit: Phillips Family Archives.

Former Choate Headmaster Seymour St. John celebrating
Dave's sixtieth birthday in Roaring Gap, North Carolina.
Photo Credit: Courtesy of John and Pat Bassett.

Dave and Kay meet the Dalai Lama on the Smithsonian Institution's board trip to India. Photo Credit: Courtesy of Smithsonian Institute.

Kay kissed by a giraffe when the Phillips family traveled to Nairobi, Kenya. Photo Credit: Phillips Family Archive.

US Ambassador Dave Phillips and Estonian chief of protocol review the troops in front of the presidential palace. Photo Credit: US Embassy.

Ambassador Dave Phillips and his wife, Kay, greeting Turkish Prime Minister Recep Tayyip Erdogan in Estonia in 2008.
Photo Credit: US State Department.

US Marine Guards march during the Independence Day Celebration in Estonia in front of the residence of Ambassador Dave and Kay Phillips. Photo Credit: US Embassy.

Ambassador Dave Phillips walks with Vice President Cheney, President Ilves of Estonia, and President Bush at the White House in 2007. Photo Credit: US State Department.

Ambassador Dave Phillips talks with President Bush while leaving the Oval
Office during a visit to the White House in 2007.
Photo Credit: US State Department.

Louis Quijas, former assistant director of the FBI and former police chief
of High Point, North Carolina, with Robert Mueller, former director of the
FBI, and Kay Phillips and Ambassador Dave Phillips, in Estonia.
Photo Credit: US State Department.

A photo of the USS Enterprise that received Ambassador Phillips, President Ilves, and government officials from Estonia in the Mediterranean in 2008. Photo Credit: US Navy Department.

Kay and Dave Phillips greeting Condoleezza Rice at Valleyfields Farm in High Point, North Carolina, after she spoke at the Ambassador Dave and Kay Phillips Family International Lecture Series at Duke University in 2012. Photo Credit: Phillips Family Archives.

Mitt Romney, former governor of Massachusetts and Republican presidential candidate, with Kay and Dave Phillips at Duke University in 2013 for the Ambassador Dave and Kay Phillips Family International Lecture Series. Photo Credit: Duke University.

# CHAPTER 16

## *Bringing People Together*

A s Market Square was expanding, so was Dave's involvement with other businesses in the region.

Dave explained that High Point's economic development strategy took an upbeat turn when internationally known motivational speaker and businessman Tom Haggai formed a group of local CEOs.

"Tom had become aware that other cities in America had organized their leadership to help their communities. He invited a small group of us to meet together, representing different experiences from the civic and business community. Interestingly, Tom had started his career as a Baptist minister, then became known nationally as an inspirational speaker before being named the Chairman of IGA (International Grocers Alliance), which brought him into international prominence," said Dave.

Their mission was to help High Point, as the business community had had little interaction with city government. It became apparent to the CEO group that a relationship needed to be created with the political and governmental leadership in High Point so they could easily work together.

Dave helped achieve this cohesiveness locally through the re-establishment of the High Point Economic Development Corporation and the creation of the High Point Partnership. The High Point Economic Development Corporation board had half of its members from government and the other half from business. Dave was elected the first chairman.

That was when Dave began championing the cause of regionalism throughout the area and throughout the state. He recognized that, through collaboration and cooperation, the concept of regionalism could provide an economic boon. That would prove easy to theorize but much more difficult in practice as leaders naturally try to protect their own turf.

To that end, the Piedmont Triad Development Corporation was created. The president of Wake Forest University represented Winston-Salem, a former mayor of Greensboro represented Greensboro, and Dave represented High Point. These three leaders invited five CEOs from each city to all meet together. They were amazed to discover that some of these CEOs had never met each other. "We were just astonished," Dave said as he explained that one would think that CEOs of major corporations would have met on several occasions. "We all realized that the region needed to work together for economic development."

"Location. Transportation. Workforce. Quality of life. Every region is measured by what it offers its citizens and corporate investors. The twelve-county Piedmont Triad region of North Carolina is a region of rich resources and vast potential. The Piedmont Triad offers an excellent location, superior education, a strong arts community, and a corporate community that has embraced and invested in the region," he said.

One project the Piedmont Triad Development Corporation decided to tackle was the name of the airport. Its current name was the Greensboro Winston-Salem High Point Regional Airport, which was a mouthful for anyone.

"There was a unanimous decision to call it Piedmont Triad Airport, which made perfect sense. The new airport name would be the symbol of us working together as a region.

"One board member said, 'I've got another idea. Let's call it international.'"

They discovered that the airport did, indeed, have a few international flights, so they submitted the application to change the name of the airport to Piedmont Triad International—and it was approved.

"We then tried to change the airport code to PTI from GSO, but the FAA made it very clear, very quickly, that was not going to be accepted."

In a 1988 interview, Dave explained the concept of the change: "The airport is the gateway to future cooperation as manifested in the groups now meeting together—the Chambers, the elected officials, city and county administrators. This is our growth area. Each city has its own personality, but we need to help each other."

Dave emphasized that change is "very positive. It opens up all kinds of marketing opportunities for the whole region."

In my later research, I discovered that an interviewer, Sharon Kilby, made the comment, "With characteristic enthusiasm, Phillips makes the area sound as alluring as a South Seas Island, as exciting as New York City, and as ripe with potential as an undeveloped nation."

"We learned during this time that the greater Triad was more dynamic than three individual cities, and the interchange of commerce and communities in a region of twelve counties should be tied together. The approach was very similar to the High Point Partnership in that elected officials, government leaders, and the business community needed to strategize and communicate the capabilities of the region and not be selfish to their neighborhood," explained Dave. To that end, twelve counties were incorporated into the Piedmont Triad Partnership.

"We met regularly at seven thirty in the morning in different locations in the region. This took real dedication; believe it or not, everybody showed up. The idea was to allow counties and cities to get to know each other and to work together."

Dave recalled one particularly amusing incident. "Several of us had gone to Hardees to get coffee, and when we returned to the Kernersville Public Library for our meeting that morning, my leg came off, and coffee went everywhere. I had to pull down my pants to put my leg back on. A very prominent person was on his knees in front of me trying to clean up the mess when two ladies opened the front door and took one look and ran out the door."

Even though each Chamber of Commerce tended to advocate for its individual city, people in their twelve counties all needed jobs. So, the twelve counties endeavored to work together for the common cause, to get jobs for their constituents. Dave recalled, "It became more and more important to market the twelve counties as a region. Companies could draw on the infrastructure of education, roads, and a larger employment base. The Piedmont Triad Partnership was the ideal conduit."

Over time, North Carolina governmental leaders took notice of Dave's successes in business and his increased involvement in bringing business leaders together in the Piedmont Triad region.

When Governor Jim Martin asked Dave to serve on the North Carolina Board of Transportation in the late 1980s, Dave answered, "I would be honored to."

As a member of the Board of Transportation, Dave promoted two projects for his hometown that have improved the traffic flow and have impacted the lives of High Pointers, as I knew very well.

The first project concerned High Point College (now High Point University). At the time, it was an intimate college campus with the exception of one obstacle. A road, Montlieu Avenue, divided the campus. A road running through the middle of the campus was not only disruptive to the students and faculty, but it was dangerous for people to cross the busy thoroughfare. Dave supported the initiative to reroute Montlieu Avenue and unite the campus, and the project received funding.

Today, due to the continued expansion of the campus, that one-mile stretch of Montlieu has been closed to the public to accommodate the expansion of the university, including three additional academic buildings in the health and science fields of study.

The other initiative that Dave is proud to have supported is referred to as R-2606B, which created the US 311 Bypass. For decades, High Pointers had talked of a bypass. As the city continued to grow, traffic congestion on US 311 through Main Street became more congested, making travel through High Point very difficult. One of the benefits of being on the North Carolina Board of Transportation is that a member may campaign for a transportation issue concerning their district. Dave took that opportunity to champion the US 311 Bypass, also known as US 74.

In the early 1990s, in the tight state budget, there was just a limited amount of money to negotiate for and to distribute around the state. The US 311/US 74 bypass was a massive project budgeted at over $125 million. It was easy to put the plan on paper but not so easy to get it added to the official docket of the Transportation Improvement Program (TIP). Once on the list, however, the project was funded.

After almost twenty-five years in the making, the US 311/US 74 Bypass is now completed. "Now it is more than just a dream," Dave said. Interestingly, the High Point mayor wrote a letter to the Department of Transportation about naming the US 311/US 74 Bypass after Dave, but, unfortunately, they had just changed the rules and regulations of naming highways for individual persons.

I sat back in my chair and allowed all the dots to connect. "It seems that serving your community has always gone hand in hand with whatever financial success you had.

"That also plays into not having enemies but only opposition, right? In terms of bringing competing business leaders together in your region, you wanted everyone to be successful—not just your company, but your town, your region, and your state."

"Well, that's right," Dave said. "Everything I've done in my life is bringing people together. And I think that's what Governor Hunt noticed, too—which leads me to another story."

# CHAPTER 17

# North Carolina Secretary of Commerce

I remembered that after serving his first two terms as governor of North Carolina, Hunt had made a bid to run for the office of US senator against the formidable incumbent Jesse Helms. Dave had not only supported Helms but also held a very successful fundraiser at his High Point home for him.

Eight years later, in 1992, Hunt decided to make a bid for his third term as governor of North Carolina and won.

The day before Thanksgiving in 1992, Governor-elect Hunt made a telephone call to Dave, asking him to meet with him in Raleigh the day after Thanksgiving.

Dave said the telephone call from Governor-elect Hunt was one of the most intriguing calls of his career, and their meeting proved even more memorable. Governor Hunt wanted to interview Dave to serve as secretary of commerce.

"We met the day after Thanksgiving in his law office. I didn't know him very well but was honored to be there. I thought we would talk for about an hour, but we talked for several hours.

"We really hit it off right away. He wanted to know about our economic efforts in High Point and in the Piedmont Triad. He wanted to talk about regionalism, and we had a terrific conversation about economic development in North Carolina."

Three weeks later, Dave was asked to serve as the secretary of commerce for North Carolina.

"What's particularly interesting is that I had raised money for two Republican presidents, and I had worked for a Republican governor. Governor Hunt was a Democrat. But the governor loved the idea of regionalism, and I think it's one of the main reasons he asked me to work for him."

Those who knew Dave at the time also knew that he was continuing a tradition started by his father. After announcing his appointment as North Carolina secretary of commerce, a 1992 article published in the *High Point Enterprise* stated,

> Phillips inherited a sense of commitment to public issues. His father, Earl N. Phillips Sr., was mayor of High Point in the 1940s. Like his father, Dave Phillips knows that part of earning a good living means building a better community.
>
> That kind of commitment often requires personal sacrifice, and Phillips is giving up a lot by setting aside his business interests for a job in state government. High Point and the Triad are losing something, too. Of course, High Point gains by placing one of its leading citizens high in state government. But Phillips isn't only an advocate of High Point or the Triad anymore. He now assumes a larger role and all of North Carolina will benefit. Everyone knows that Hunt is a smart politician. Now, by appointing Phillips, that speculation had proven to be true.

I shared this article with Dave. "What did that mean, 'setting aside your business interests?'"

"Well, I would need to work full time in this position. Fortunately, I had terrific associates, and they could easily continue to manage the companies."

During Hunt's campaign, he stated that the most important areas for growth would be education and economic development. Dave had been a perfect choice for Hunt since he had been known statewide and nationally as an active supporter of the arts, the state zoo, medical centers, universities, and sports projects. As a member of the state Board of Transportation, Dave was well aware of the relationship between roads, education, health care, recreation, and quality of life issues in regard to economic development.

"I felt so fortunate to join Hunt's administration as secretary of commerce. He thought that regionalism would dramatically help the state and create jobs. The North Carolina Partnership was soon formed, and it was composed of public and private leadership. All one hundred counties would be organized into seven different regions. The idea was that prospective clients from around the world could easily evaluate seven regions versus one hundred counties in the state. Historically, the rural areas of the state had been overlooked and didn't have the resources to attract industry, much less to compete. The driving force for regions was to create a level field for all citizens of North Carolina to have an opportunity for a job."

Dave obviously loved his state of North Carolina; he had proven salesmanship ability, especially when the product was his home state. "North Carolina has a lot to market. It isn't just the beautiful land, the seashore, and the mountains. It's the economic diversity.

"Governor Hunt knew what we were doing in the Triad, and so, the governor and I did the same thing for the state of North Carolina."

This concept was also a natural progression for Dave since he and his Market Square Partners had traveled all over the world trying to entice the furniture industry to invest in High Point, North Carolina.

"Once you have the attention of economic development prospects, you must present all possibilities of the entire state," Dave explained. "There are approximately 500 communities spread over 100 counties in North Carolina. Everybody wants economic development.

"The state is like a shopping mall. Large cities are major stores, and the small towns are boutiques. Everybody cooperates, and we endeavor to make it easy shopping for prospective clients.

"Eventually, all the communities felt comfortable being in one of seven regions. They'd consider their traffic patterns, their commuting patterns, their medical facilities, and their schools, and they'd conclude, 'Yes, we're in this region over here.' They knew that it would work because it's what they did already in their daily lives."

Dave would encounter his first challenge marketing North Carolina commerce shortly after accepting the position. North Carolina provided everything a business could want, and that is what Governor Hunt hoped when he discovered that the German automobile maker Mercedes-Benz wanted to open an assembly plant in the United States.

The word of this new venture in America prompted the courtship of states throughout the country to try to attract the company to their area. North Carolina was no exception. At this time, in 1993, Governor Hunt wanted to recruit a car manufacturing plant, just like South Carolina had done with BMW. North Carolina was already home to several truck manufacturers, but the car industry was not represented.

As soon as Governor Hunt found out the intentions of Mercedes-Benz, he turned to Dave and told him, "Dave, we have to get this. I want you to get your best people on it. Let's find out what Mercedes-Benz needs. Let's do everything we can to get this plant in North Carolina."

They contacted Mercedes-Benz and asked what it would take for them to come to North Carolina. Mercedes-Benz mentioned the work force and then stressed the point that this project would not be incentive-driven. This statement ultimately proved to be more fiction than fact.

The Mercedes-Benz plant quickly became the number one economic development project in the United States. Almost every state in America wanted Mercedes-Benz.

The governor and Dave were very pleased when it was made public that North Carolina had been put on the "short list" of potential states. The others were South Carolina and Alabama. There were many meetings and presentations with Mercedes-Benz about North Carolina roads, airports, education, power rates and utilities, housing, training, and status as a right-to-work state, meaning non-union.

Then there was a trip to New York that was most memorable. At four o'clock on a Thursday afternoon, Dave received a phone call telling him that the CEO of Mercedes-Benz was flying in from the headquarters in Stuttgart to New York the following Monday. It was imperative that all three, Governor Hunt, Senator Helms, and Dave, be at the Seagram Building on Park Avenue in New York City to advance to the next round. Bill Lee, chairman of the North Carolina Economic Board and CEO of Duke Energy, was also invited on the trip.

Hunt asked Dave to make the phone call to Helms. He did. Helms had another appointment for Monday, but he realized the importance of the New York meeting and said to Dave, "Can I call you back in fifteen minutes?" Helms changed the appointment so he could fly with Hunt and Dave to New York for the meeting with Mercedes-Benz International.

The flight to New York took on a historical noteworthiness. The former political rivals put aside their differences to become allies to promote their beloved state of North Carolina. Dave recalled that day, and the memory of the camaraderie and courtesies between Helms and Hunt was almost inspiring: "They talked about their families and what had transpired in their lives and what they both could do to help North Carolina. They were both very impressive as they made the North Carolina presentation to the leaders of Mercedes-Benz."

South Carolina already had successfully lured the BMW plant to its state and knew that the infrastructure around the plant was of importance. Consideration of suppliers for the automobile companies was one of those issues. As it turned out, those issues were not the primary concern on which a decision would be based.

"We soon learned that South Carolina was no longer being considered. It was going to be a competition between North Carolina and Alabama. We also learned that it was going to be 'incentive-driven' and not based on the most educated work force or the best infrastructure."

The incentive package North Carolina put together totaled about $100 million. "It was the highest of any package that had ever been put together in North Carolina.

"In the end, Alabama offered a half a billion in incentives, and Alabama got the plant."

Still, both Hunt and Dave looked at the process as a real learning experience. They learned that companies may say incentives are not important, but at the end of the day, incentives do make a difference.

Although North Carolina lost the Mercedes-Benz plant to Alabama in 1993, because of the way the Mercedes-Benz negotiations were handled, the reputation of North Carolina is highly regarded around the world.

# CHAPTER 18

# Marketing North Carolina to the World

As they continued to sell North Carolina throughout the world, Governor
Hunt and Dave shared many adventures in their frequent travels.

One trip took them to Israel to meet with Prime Minister Rabin.
Governor Hunt formed a delegation to travel to Israel since many Israeli
companies had investments in North Carolina. El Al Israel Airlines, the flagship
carrier of Israel, arranged to have one of its planes pick them up in Raleigh-
Durham for the flight to Israel. Security on the flight and the entire trip was very
tight. The delegation enjoyed staying at one of the world's most storied hotels,
King David, a famous landmark in Jerusalem.

In the fall of 1995, they met separately with both Prime Minister Rabin and
former Prime Minister Netanyahu, who would regain that position in 2009.
At the time, Netanyahu was the leader of the opposition for the Likud Party.
Dave discovered he and Netanyahu shared a similar interest. Although briefly,
Netanyahu had been the chief marketing officer for a furniture company in Israel
before pursuing his political career.

The next day, they met with Prime Minister Rabin in his cabinet room.
Rabin spoke about the missiles launched at Israel during the Gulf War in the

early 1990s and how the United States had sent anti-missiles to Israel for its defense. Rabin did express concern about his safety, fearing that there would be an assassination attempt on his life.

His worst fears were realized only two weeks later when he was walking down the steps of city hall. It is speculated that a radical right-wing assassin killed Rabin because of his signing of the Oslo Accords, which, ironically, earned him the Nobel Peace Prize.

A year later, they took a trip to South Africa. On the way, a delegation from North Carolina stopped in Zimbabwe because of the tobacco industry connection: Zimbabwe was one of the world's largest producers and exporters of tobacco.

While in Zimbabwe, Governor Hunt and Dave met with the tobacco industrialists but also had an appointment to meet with the controversial president of Zimbabwe, Robert Mugabe. As they waited in the anteroom, they could hear the president speaking in his office. They kept waiting and waiting and began to read the magazines that were on the coffee table. They noticed a peculiar commonality. Each one had a similar theme . . . the magazines were from North Korea, China, and Russia. The common thread was that they promoted Communism. According to Dave, he and Hunt felt slightly uneasy and commented between themselves about the Communist magazines.

The receptionist overheard the comments concerning the magazines, took notice, and in his very British accent said, "Gentlemen, do not despair. When the Communists come here, we put out *Forbes, Business Week,* and *Fortune.*" They laughed, and even though the chill in the air didn't quite turn to warmth, the ice was, indeed, broken as they waited for the president to emerge.

After they had waited in the reception area for a considerable length of time, the door to the presidential office opened. There was President Mugabe, sitting at a large desk on a raised platform. As Mugabe looked down upon Dave and the governor, they attempted to talk about the relationship of the tobacco companies. "Jim Hunt did a masterful job talking about the state of North Carolina to Mugabe," Dave recalled and added, "We were as polite as possible and concluded our meeting."

The next stop was South Africa. This was shortly after Nelson Mandela had been elected president in 1994. The delegation had hoped to meet with the newly elected president, but he was out of the country. Instead, they met with Nobel Peace Prize recipient Archbishop Desmond Tutu and former South African president, Frederik Willem de Klerk, who, with Nelson Mandela, is renowned for engineering the end of apartheid.

The meeting was very interesting and extended beyond the scope of economics as de Klerk openly spoke about his strong feelings against apartheid and his hopes for a smooth passage from racial segregation as Mandela assumed the country's presidency. De Klerk made it clear that he fully supported the black community's involvement in the leadership of South Africa and that it would ensure a hopeful future.

De Klerk proved to be right in his assessment of the integration of South Africa; however, the smooth transition that was initially hoped for did not come to fruition.

"We were fortunate to be in South Africa during a very historical time," added Dave.

In addition, on their trade mission trips, Hunt and Dave traveled to Europe, Asia, and the Middle East, meeting other world leaders such as Prime Minister Murayama of Japan and President Zedillo of Mexico.

"We not only traveled internationally, but we would also go to Hollywood and sell North Carolina to the film industry. Dino De Laurentiis had his film studio in Wilmington, and we were becoming known as one of the premier states for filmmaking. We had great locations and a supportive infrastructure, and it was creating jobs. So, we would go to California and have receptions to meet producers, directors, and actors and encourage them to come to North Carolina."

One notable story involved a producer who came to North Carolina to make a motion picture at Biltmore House, the largest private home in the United States, built in the late 1800s for George and Edith Vanderbilt. The historic estate, in the mountains of Asheville, was the perfect place for producer Joel Silver to make a film adaptation of *Richie Rich*, based on the Harvey Comics comic book character Richie Rich, the world's wealthiest kid. The 1994 film starred Macaulay Culkin in his final film as a child actor. Silver had produced the first two *Die Hard* films and the *Lethal Weapon* series, all enormously successful. Silver was famous in the film industry for his colorful language, having been interviewed regularly in the trade magazines. What a coup it was to have a big-time producer like Silver come to North Carolina!

However, things were rocky from the start with the fiery producer. The trouble began with the negotiations to film on location at Biltmore House. The owner did not want the film crew to have access to Biltmore until the last tour of the day was completed. He also wanted the film crew to be completely out when Biltmore opened each morning. This was just not enough time for a day's shooting. Silver was offering an enormous sum of money, but the conditions for filming at Biltmore House remained the same. It reached the point where negotiations had totally stalled.

Dave received a phone call from Silver saying that he was upset and was taking *Richie Rich* to England to film, where there were more than enough expansive estates to shoot the film. Silver said, in very colorful language, that he could no longer deal with Biltmore House. The situation quickly escalated to the point that North Carolina seemed destined to lose the film, the money, and the recognition it had hoped to gain.

Dave remembers the delicacy of the situation. He and Governor Hunt were in Charlotte for a meeting. They were in the back seat of a highway patrol car talking about issues to discuss that day, and the Joel Silver movie was on the agenda. Dave proceeded to tell the governor about the phone call from Silver and the tenuous predicament concerning the negotiation for Biltmore House. The governor asked Dave to recount the telephone call. Dave hesitated but then told the governor, word for word, what Silver had said, including the long string of profanities. Both the patrolman and the State Bureau of Investigation agent both started to laugh as the patrol car swerved.

"Governor Hunt, who did not use profanity, turned to me, looked me in the eye, and said, 'Dave, you handle it.'" Eventually, *Richie Rich* was filmed at the historic Biltmore Estate, and the owner was paid very handsomely. Unfortunately, the film's reviews did not fare as well.

North Carolina began to focus more on California, hoping to lure other West Coast businesses—in addition to film projects—to the state. The focus was so successful that North Carolina opened a recruiting office in California for economic developers. In other words, there were so many inquiries from the state of California that it was deemed economically advantageous to set up an office instead of flying recruiters back and forth. It was the first time any state had opened an office in another state to attract business and industry. This maneuver was not well received by the state of California, however.

Later in his term, Dave, along with secretaries of commerce from several other states, including California, were invited to cruise up the Hudson River to West Point on the *Highlander* yacht, owned by billionaire Malcolm Forbes. The chairman of Forbes Inc., Caspar Weinberger, former secretary of defense under President Reagan, was also on the cruise. While aboard the yacht, Dave was seated next to the acting deputy secretary of the California Trade and Commerce Agency.

"She became very upset when she found out I was from North Carolina," said Dave. "Governor Hunt and I had just recently gone on an industry-hunting trip to California and an article had appeared in the *Los Angeles Times*. We garnered a certain amount of notoriety because of the office we opened in California to encourage companies to leave California and bring their business to North Carolina. She was not pleased!

"Jim Hunt used to say that the number one social program is 'JOBS.' My job was trying to create and retain jobs, and, as a businessperson, I could relate to that. If you really are going to help the people of North Carolina, it takes major programs and tremendous support to make things happen. Jim Hunt did that.

"The Hunt days were fabulous. We had a lot of fun, and we traveled the world. We met fascinating people and were also able to implement many economic development projects."

Although Dave had a great time while serving as secretary of commerce, he also admitted that at times it was hard: he had to live in a hotel during the week while Kay remained at home in High Point with two of their four daughters who had not gone off to school.

Toward the end of Dave's tenure as secretary of commerce, he and Governor Hunt launched a novel plan concerning North Carolina's future negotiations to attract companies to all areas of the state. North Carolina would provide incentives through the newly established North Carolina Economic Development Commission. They developed a set of what the governor felt were appropriate incentives without "giving away the store." The William S. Lee Quality Jobs and Business Expansion Act, known commonly as the Bill Lee Act of 1996, created tax credits for job creation, investment, and worker training. This act was named for former Duke Energy Chairman William States Lee III, who had been chairman of the North Carolina Economic Development Board.

After Lee died of a heart attack, Governor Hunt appointed Dave as his successor as chairman. This appointment occurred as Dave completed his four-year term in Hunt's cabinet, in 1997.

"What stands out the most to you about those years?" I asked.

Dave thought for a moment. "The fact that I was asked to work for the Democratic governor of North Carolina. I had supported Republicans, like Helms, Reagan, and Bush, so it was surprising to a lot of people. It shows that he had enough confidence coming back as governor where he just wanted to get on with helping his state. That was really big on his part, I thought.

"During this time, I was also asked to run by both Republicans and Democrats for political office. I was always honored, but I had witnessed frustrations with trying to create change in business and politics. However, I think every citizen has the responsibility to participate in their community, in business, and in government.

"Let me share with you a saying that always makes me laugh. It applies to both politics and business."

Dave handed me a piece of paper with the following words:

### The Plan

*In the beginning was the plan,*
*And then came the assumptions,*
*And the assumptions were without form,*
*And the plan was, therefore, without substance.*

*And darkness was on the face of the multitude,*
*And they spoke among themselves, saying,*
*"It is a crock of sh\*\*, and it stinketh."*
*And the staff members went to the multitude and sayeth,*
*"It is a pile of dung, and none may abide the odor thereof."*
*And the staff members went to the divisions and sayeth unto them,*
*"It is a container of excrement, and it is so strong that none may abide it."*
*And the divisions went to the department managers and sayeth unto them,*
*"It is a vessel of fertilizer, and none may abide its strength."*
*And the department managers went to the directors and sayeth,*
*"It contains that which aids growth, and it is very strong."*
*And the directors went to the vice presidents and sayeth,*
*"It promoteth growth, and it is very powerful."*
*And the vice presidents went to the president and sayeth unto him,*
*"This powerful new plan will actively promote the growth, strength, and*
*efficiency of the institution."*
*And the president looked upon the plan and saw that it was good,*
*And the plan became policy.*

# CHAPTER 19

# *The Special Olympics*

While serving as secretary of commerce in 1996, Dave was approached by the Special Olympics of North Carolina, who posed the question, "Why don't we make a bid to bring the Special Olympics World Games to North Carolina?" Dave was immediately intrigued with the proposal.

Kay had a young friend with special needs, and their friendship had made Dave aware of the Special Olympics, although he did not realize its magnitude, both nationally and internationally. As Dave learned more about the Special Olympics, he, too, became passionate about its opportunities and advocacy for those with mental challenges. His memories of his own challenges with his handicap and later amputation, coupled with his love for his home state, made Dave a perfect choice to lead the effort to bring the Special Olympics World Games to North Carolina.

The year in question was 1999, when both Ohio and Texas were also vying to host the Special Olympics. The stakes were big. If North Carolina were to be awarded the Games, it would be the largest sporting event ever held in the state. Dave had only one question, "How do we make this work?"

He decided the first step should be to meet with the Special Olympics founder, Eunice Shiver, and the chairman/CEO of the Special Olympics, Sargent Shriver. Their first meeting was in Washington, DC, even though, at the time, the Shrivers had made Chicago their home. The first International Special Olympics Games was held in Chicago at Soldier Field in 1968 with 1,000 athletes from 26 states and Canada.

Sargent Shriver, who was also the founding director of the Peace Corps, had managed the Merchandise Mart in Chicago for the Kennedy family.

At the first meeting with the Shrivers, Dave posed the question, "What does North Carolina need to do to get the Special Olympics World Games?" The answer was easily summed up as follows: "It would take emotion and passion, but it would also take money, a lot of money." North Carolina needed to provide housing, food, and transportation for both athletes and chaperones.

The directness and magnitude of that response simply gave Dave more resolve to bring the Special Olympics to North Carolina.

In a 1998 article featured in *Business Life*, Dave was described as the "tallest soldier, spending most of his waking moments building the case to convince the Special Olympics committee to bestow this great honor [of hosting the Special Olympics] on North Carolina."

With the collaboration and support of Duke University and North Carolina Central University in Durham, North Carolina State University in the capital of Raleigh, and the University of North Carolina at Chapel Hill, Dave realized that his dream and the dream of other North Carolinians could become a reality. The four universities—with sporting facilities, dormitories for lodging, and dining areas—could provide the infrastructure needed to accommodate the athletes, trainers, coaches, and chaperones.

With the four institutions located so closely together in the region known as the Research Triangle, Dave convinced the committee that North Carolina had tremendous infrastructure to offer. Sargent was very impressed with Dave's determination, and with North Carolina. But it wouldn't be that easy. Sargent told Dave that he needed a commitment and a pledge of $5 million by the end of the week. Dave's response to Sargent was, "We will raise the money."

Now Dave was even more determined to succeed. With Governor Hunt, Dave wasted no time beginning the campaign. They called upon executives Hugh McColl and Ken Lewis at NationsBank (now Bank of America) and made their presentation. "You have the name. You have the reputation. Would you be the corporate sponsor for the Special Olympics?" The answer was an overwhelming yes. The condition of raising $5 million by the end of the week was met.

Dave then contacted his long-time friend, Jesse Helms.

"I said, 'Senator, we need your help. The Kennedy family has made it clear that they don't want to ask the federal government for help with the Special Olympics World Games.'" The Kennedy family did not feel comfortable using the family name as a source of funding. But Dave stressed to his friend that "We, as North Carolina, need help. We will have athletes from over 150 countries, and we need support and security. We need the federal government to help us."

Senator Helms's first reaction was jocular: "Goodness gracious! I will help you, but do I have to negotiate with Ted Kennedy?" Then Helms responded more seriously as he invited his friend to Washington, DC, to lobby for the state of North Carolina. Dave, with the support of Helms, Senator Lauch Faircloth, and former White House deputy chief of staff, Erskine Bowles, knocked on door after door, asking for help.

Dave proved to be very convincing, and several different branches of the federal government offered $15 million for the infrastructure, making the total committed so far $20 million. Other corporate sponsors jumped on the Special Olympics bandwagon for a total of more than $35 million. North Carolina secured the 1999 Special Olympics.

Dave's previous experience in business, economic partnerships, and regionalism all were advantageous as Dave chaired the 1999 Special Olympics. Over 36,000 volunteers were recruited to serve the 7,000 athletes from 150 nations.

Dave still had work to do. He approached fellow High Pointer and friend Tom Haggai, president of IGA (Independent Grocers Alliance), about donating food to the Games. In turn, IGA donated over $2 million in food to the event. Other donations solicited by Dave included $2 million by Sara Lee for the athletic and volunteer uniforms and $1 million from Lowe's. In addition, Jefferson Pilot, the accounting firm Arthur Andersen, and the law firm Smith, Helms, Mulliss & Moore all donated services each worth over $500,000. GlaxoSmithKline donated $1 million and 1,000 of their employees as volunteers.

The expectation of hosting the Special Olympics created major excitement throughout the state of North Carolina.

As the planning and preparation for the Games began, Dave asked Arnold Palmer and Michael Jordan to be co-chairmen. Both athletes hold a sentimental affection for North Carolina. Palmer graduated from Wake Forest University, and the new Arnold Palmer Golf Complex had been dedicated in his honor. Jordan grew up in North Carolina and played basketball at the University of North Carolina. Both accepted the distinction of honorary co-chairmen.

Just as with the regular Olympics, the Olympic Torch is the symbol of the Special Olympics and is lit before the opening ceremony at the site of the ancient Olympics in Olympia, Greece. It is said that Jackie Kennedy Onassis used her influence to persuade the Greek government to carry on the Olympic torch tradition with the Special Olympics. Dave flew to Greece for the age-old ceremony.

"I arrived in Greece, and, unfortunately, Kay was unable to travel with me as she usually did. They ushered me in a Rolls Royce limousine with motorcycles in front and back as an escort, with lights and sirens blaring. I was all by myself, and I'm reasoning that if I tell this story, no one is going to believe me."

The next day, he and the Special Olympians were presented the Olympic Torch on Mt. Olympus for the Special Olympics World Games in North Carolina.

That night the American ambassador to Greece invited Dave to the Embassy for dinner, and he was seated next to the Jordanian ambassador to Greece, the step-brother of the reigning king of Jordan, King Abdullah II bin al-Hussein, son of the late King Hussein and Princess Muna al-Hussein. The dinner conversation was interesting but took a decidedly more interesting turn when the Jordanian ambassador mentioned that he had attended Deerfield Academy in New England. Deerfield is the archrival of Choate.

The conversation immediately changed from chitchat to a friendly competitive banter. To the students at Choate, Deerfield students and alumni were called "green weenies" because of their school color of green and their green shirts and outfits.

As Dave divulged that he had attended Choate, the ambassador quickly responded, "Oh, you are a Choatie."

Dave, not to be outdone, said, "Oh, my gosh. You are a green weenie!"

The ambassador, not to be outdone said, "You know the King of Jordan went to Deerfield, too."

Dave continued the repartee. "I guess he's a green weenie, too."

"Are you calling my king a green weenie?" the ambassador countered.

"I guess I am," answered Dave.

When the Jordanian plane landed at the Raleigh-Durham International Airport for the Special Olympics, Kay and Dave were there to greet them. First off the plane were the athletes and then the Jordanian ambassador, who immediately spotted Dave.

"I told the king you called him a green weenie," he said.

"What did he say?" Dave asked.

"The king was pissed," was the answer.

In fact, King Abdullah thought so highly of his years at Deerfield that he was inspired to help found King's Academy in Madaba, Jordan, a college preparatory school fashioned after his beloved Deerfield.

Back in North Carolina, the finishing touches were being put into place. North Carolina communities offered unprecedented and enthusiastic support for the Special Olympics and in welcoming the special athletes.

Many communities throughout North Carolina adopted and hosted different countries, providing housing and helping the athletes adjust to the jetlag. This created a special bond in the towns and cities and emotionally tied North Carolinians together. Volunteers even had to be turned away. They couldn't accept more than 36,000, and many of those needed to be in skilled positions to manage the different facilities.

There was also the logistical challenge of transportation to and from various sporting venues. In the sports world, that is called a true team effort. This event was so monumental that it was the largest combined sporting event in the world that year. Since the North Carolina Special Olympics in 1999, the international summer games have literally traveled the world, to Ireland in 2003, to China in 2007, to Greece in 2011, and in 2015, the Special Olympics returned to America and were held in Los Angeles, California.

That team effort also included what was called "the largest peacetime airlift in the history of America." The Citation Special Olympics Airlift organized the effort by contacting all Citation owners and asking them to transport a team from their area. Two hundred and seventy-five private jets were donated to pick up over 2,000 members on the USA Special Olympic team all over the United States. The FAA even gave the Special Olympics a special call sign to track them across the country as traffic controllers around the country knew the importance of their arrival at their designated time slot. That schedule was reversed two weeks later, returning the American athletes to their hometowns. It was a monumental effort physically and emotionally as many of the athletes had never flown in any kind of plane before . . . much less a private plane. More than 55,000 athletes, volunteers, and spectators attended the opening ceremony.

At the start of the Games, Billy Graham delivered the invocation, and Maya Angelou recited a poem. Dave had visited the distinguished author at her Winston-Salem home to ask her personally to participate in the Special Olympics. She read a special version of her poem "Still I Rise" for the Opening Ceremony, entitled "I Rise! A Tribute to Special Olympics," which captured the spirit of the Special Olympians.

Several years later, Tim Shriver, the current chairman of the Special Olympics, sent Dave a copy of the script of her inspiring words. Dave handed it to me, and I saw that Shriver had included a personal note:

> The great poet and novelist Maya Angelou stood before the athletes of the Special Olympics at the opening ceremonies of the World Summer Games in North Carolina and shared with them, and with the world, the beauty of our movement. I read her words and realized their timelessness and power. I hope they will inspire you as much as they inspire me.

Angelou's words continue to inspire, especially the last few lines: "Just like hope springing high, still I rise. I may be small, smaller than you. I may be tall, taller than you. I may be fat. I may be thin. I may be plain. I may be pretty. I may be cute according to the fashion and still I rise. I rise! I rise!"

Pride and grandeur reverberated throughout the world as, one by one, the special delegations from 150 countries walked behind their flags to the cheers of the 55,000 attendees filling the stadium to capacity.

The opening ceremonies for the ten-day event were held at Carter-Finley Stadium on the campus of North Carolina State University in the capital city of Raleigh. Billy Crystal served as the emcee for the gala opening ceremony. His most noteworthy quip, which played well with North Carolinians, was, "Not many people know that Coach Krzyzewski's name is worth 10,000 points in Scrabble."

Arnold and Maria Schwarzenegger sat and cheered among the crowd with their children. "Everyone loved Arnold, and he enjoyed spending time talking with his fans, with his big cigar in his mouth. The US Navy's Blue Angels paid tribute as they flew across the blue Carolina skies," recalled Dave.

Stevie Wonder entertained with many of his songs, including the heartfelt "You Are the Sunshine of My Life." After his performance, the Phillips family visited with him in his dressing room. He was very friendly and told the family about a near-fatal car accident that occurred in 1973 as he and his cousin traveled from Greenville, South Carolina, to Durham, North Carolina. Wonder lapsed into a coma, and he credited Wake Forest Baptist Medical Center with saving his life. Dave, who served on the board of trustees for the medical center, took great pleasure from the comments of the very famous patient.

Kathy Ireland, former model, actress, and entrepreneur, attended. There were also former Olympian gymnasts Nadia Comaneci and Bart Conner, and Olympic swimmer Donna de Varona. De Varona was the youngest member of the US Olympic Team that competed in the 1960 games in Rome, Italy. Later, de Varona became the first female network sportscaster, at the tender age of seventeen, and won a total of eighteen gold medals. De Varona and her husband, John Pinto, became close friends with Kay and Dave and would visit them several times while Dave was the US ambassador to Estonia.

Jon Bon Jovi, such a dear friend of the Shrivers that he referred to Eunice as "The Tornado," was not officially on the entertainment roster, but he attended the Special Olympics and delighted his fans with impromptu performances. Known as a family man, he was surrounded by his family, who had accompanied him.

Special Olympics founder Eunice Shriver delivered the welcoming speech, and her concluding words epitomize the meaning of the Special Olympics:

> You are teaching all nations the healing power of the human spirit. You are demonstrating to the entire world that disabled people are not unable and that each and every person on our planet deserves a full and fair chance to make the very most of their own ability. My heart is full this evening to see the countless miracles that the families and athletes of Special Olympics have wrought. Welcome to these games, and welcome to the better world you have helped create. Thank you and God bless you.

It was ten days forever etched in the heart and minds of North Carolinians. Surprisingly, something historical occurred at the North Carolina Special Olympics. For the first time in its history, the Special Olympic Games produced a profit. The surplus was divided equally between Special Olympics North Carolina and the national Special Olympics Inc., based in Washington, DC.

The success of the 1999 Special Olympics World Games proved to be more than financial; it was spiritual. Retrospectively, Dave added, "The 1999 Special Olympics was the most emotional endeavor that I have ever experienced. I hadn't realized the impact it would have on the citizens of our state. It was also such a profound and gratifying experience for our family."

Dave knew the impact that the Special Olympics was going to have on the state, and he felt that there would be considerable national interest. He then traveled to New York to negotiate with several broadcast companies to air the 1999 Special Olympics World Games, and the result was a two-hour primetime show by CBS.

Ultimately, several years later, Dave's experience with the Olympics would prove to be a pivotal connection for future ventures in business and politics. Mitt Romney was well aware that Dave had led the very successful and profitable 1999 Special Olympic World Games.

The two shared a common bond in that Romney was selected to take over leadership of the already financially troubled 2002 Olympic Games to be held in Salt Lake City, Utah. Romney accepted the challenge and served as president and CEO of the Salt Lake Organizing Committee. His leadership turned a potential financial fiasco into a profitable event.

Their mutual experience and success stimulated conversation concerning logistics, complications, and the budget. Dave subsequently agreed to work for the 2008 Romney presidential campaign. Dave recalled visiting Romney in Boston. They went to a Boston Red Sox game, and Romney presented Dave with an autographed baseball bat that Dave has in his High Point office. Romney would also become an investor in Market Square through Bain Capital, a company in which Dave was also an investor.

Eunice Shriver was so impressed with the 1999 Olympics that she sent Dave the book *Profiles in Courage,* written by her brother John F. Kennedy. I opened the book Dave handed to me and read the enclosed letter:

> Dear Dave,
>
> There are very few times in my life when I find myself at a loss for words, but it seems that every day during the 1999 World Games something left me speechless! From the incredible support of the host towns across the state, to unparalleled dedication from local volunteers, companies, and institutions, to world-class competition and venues for all 19 sports, North Carolina hosted a sporting event that would be considered an overwhelming success by any standard.
>
> The Games never could have been the incredible event they were, however, without a strong, supportive, and influential Board of Directors. Your leadership of the Board helped to

forge the commitment and involvement of the North Carolina community in the Games, and for that I am deeply grateful.

Indeed, these Games were "All About Attitude." Not only the attitude of the self-respect and confidence that these Games provided the more than 7,000 athletes who participated, but also the attitudes and misconceptions that have been changed because of nine incredible days. North Carolina showed the world that all people, regardless of their ability, are worthy of our respect and admiration.

I hope that the enclosed will always remind you of not only the role you played in the Games' success but also the courage and abilities of our athletes that you helped make known. Thanks again for your commitment to the Games and your continued support of Special Olympics.

Affectionately,

Eunice

# CHAPTER 20

# Sale of Phillips Investments

After Dave's term as secretary of commerce ended in 1997, he was both serving as chairman of the North Carolina Economic Development Board and leading preparations for the Special Olympics. In the meantime, his businesses were continuing to run smoothly, and he anticipated returning to his role as an entrepreneur. He did, but not in the way he imagined.

Ford Motor Credit Company became interested in both Phillips Factors and Phillips Financial and approached Bob Niebauer, president of Phillips Factors Company, about purchasing the companies. Like General Motors Acceptance Corporation (GMAC) and General Electric Capital, Ford was trying to diversify their manufacturing base by expanding their financial operations. Phillips Financial was estimated to be the third largest temporary personnel finance company in America at the time.

"They had seen our presence at different venues around the country and were intrigued with the potential of the niche in the financial industry. Personnel agencies are typically small operations with very few assets other than the value of selling labor by the week and getting reimbursed by the month. We loaned money and provided computer payroll service and tax withholding information in different states in the nation. It was a unique but straightforward business opportunity and was growing rapidly."

Bob Niebauer informed Dave of the Ford Motor Credit Company inquiry. They decided to take this to their lenders, BB&T Bank and Wachovia Bank (now Wells Fargo).

"We soon learned that BB&T would be interested in purchasing us, and we negotiated and reached an agreement. This was at a time when BB&T was beginning to expand dramatically, both in assets and geography. We decided to merge in 1997, and they continue to create a solid and viable bank with outstanding leadership."

Both Phillips Factors and Phillips Financial became known as BB&T Financial. As the result of this business transaction, Dave was credited as one of the top-ten individual shareholders in the parent company, BB&T. The bank has since grown tenfold from assets of $19 billion to over $220 billion.

Just a few months later in 1997, Dave received a call from his fabric competitor, fellow High Pointer Rob Culp, who, along with his father, had founded Culp Inc., a manufacturer and global supplier of textile fabrics to the furniture industry. As competitors, they were in the same market.

Dave was recovering from a back operation when he received a surprising telephone call from Culp: "I can't believe you sold your factoring business. Would you sell your textile business?" Before the financial merger, Culp hadn't thought Dave would ever sell any of his businesses.

"I agreed to meet with him, and we did so at Valleyfields Farm. Both he and I were very worried that if we were seen together, rumors would fly; that would be to the detriment of both operations since we all knew each other. Rob had created a very successful textile company, and we understood how our operations might fit together."

Dave and Culp talked about not only the financial arrangement but also the personnel arrangement. Many of the employees had worked for Dave for years. "I wanted good futures for all of them. Rob was really good about structuring how the Phillips Textile Group would continue with Culp Inc. We put it together and basically just shook hands to make the deal."

That trust made the negotiations so much easier, and the deal was finalized in the next few months. The *High Point Enterprise* wrote, "Consolidation within the home furnishings and textile industries has prompted Culp Inc. to acquire Phillips Mills from owner S. Davis (Dave) Phillips." That article quoted Dave as saying, "Consolidations are occurring in our industry. I could see that happening, and there is a synergy between our two companies. We are compatible in most product areas, and our company is a great fit with Culp. Both companies being local, our management team knows theirs and feels comfortable with Culp. There will be no change of management except for me."

As Dave looks back on the Culp sale, he recollects that even though the timing to get out of the textile business was good, he still had many reservations about selling. "I loved being in the textile business, but within a year, the cheaper imports started pouring into this country, and it changed dramatically, not only the decorative fabrics industry but the entire textile industry. It has been devastating to the textile and the furniture business. My timing was great, but at the time neither Culp nor I had any idea that the industry was in the process of a major transformation."

After the sale of both the financial companies and his textile business, Dave contemplated what to do next. He decided to visit his friend John Mack in New York City. Mack, a fellow North Carolinian, was the chairman and chief executive officer of Morgan Stanley Company. Dave knew the Mooresville native since both families, including their children, had been involved with Duke University. Mack played football and graduated from Duke. Mack's wife, Christie, had served on the Duke Trinity Board of Trustees with Dave and had been a friend of Kay's while growing up in Greensboro.

With the proceeds from the sale to Culp Inc., Dave wanted advice on investments. While meeting with Mack at his office atop the Morgan Stanley Building in Times Square, New York, Mack posed the question to Dave, "Tell me about High Point, the International Home Furnishings Market, and your showroom complex." Dave told him about the tremendous impact that High Point had in the world, both economically and creatively, and the scope and magnitude of the showrooms.

At this time, the size of the Market Square Complex had doubled and was now about 1,050,000 square feet.

Mack asked how everything was going. Dave responded simply, "Great." Mack was intrigued and then unexpectedly asked, "Would you ever want to sell it?" Surprised at the directness of the question, Dave candidly replied, "We have never explored it." Mack explained that even though his company was primarily known for investments in stocks and bonds, Morgan Stanley was one of the largest commercial real estate sales companies in the world. The proposal piqued Dave's curiosity.

As Dave and Mack continued their discussion about High Point and Market Square, Mack requested an executive in the Real Estate Division join their conversation. The young man had just flown into New York from Hong Kong, having brokered a major office building there, and he didn't seem very impressed by a furniture showroom in High Point, North Carolina. He turned to Mack and stated, "As you know, sir, we have a minimum in the real estate division."

Mack told the young broker to get his team together and go to High Point to conduct a financial assessment. The broker turned to Dave and asked, "How do we get to High Point?" Dave said, "There are non-stop flights from New York to High Point landing at the Piedmont Triad International Airport."

The next step was for Dave to tell his partners of the John Mack meeting. Lyles was very excited about the opportunity to sell. Conversely, Froelich was not interested at all and became quite upset at the idea. Froelich had made the penthouse on the Tower his home. He and Mazie loved living there and being a part of Market Square every single day.

Dave and Lyles conversed with Froelich and finally said, "It doesn't cost anything to let the team come down here to give their evaluation as to what they think Market Square is worth." With that suggestion, Froelich acquiesced.

The team, led by the young broker, came to High Point and spent a considerable amount of time conducting a financial assessment; they returned several weeks later with their proposal. "We met at the String & Splinter Club. We were facing each other as they slid their large black binders across the table." The mood of the partners was tense as they awaited the moment of truth.

"We were nervous as we opened to the first page. Much to our relief, we were very pleased."

"As the week progressed, we learned about Real Estate Investment Trusts (REITs)," Dave explained. "This type of investment company was becoming very prominent and very successful. Morgan Stanley suggested that they evaluate several different companies.

"One of the most prominent was Vornado, the largest commercial and office real estate owner in Manhattan and in Washington, DC. One of the best aspects to us was that the Merchandise Mart in Chicago, owned by the Kennedy family, was purchased by Vornado, and they would understand and appreciate High Point and our Market Square Complex."

Even though the financial gains were measurable, Froelich was still not happy about the sale. His wife, Mazie, was more pragmatic and realized that the sale was the smart thing to do.

"Regretfully, George and Jake are no longer here, but we had a wonderful time with Market Square. My office is still in the same location in Market Square Textile Tower, where I am surrounded by great memories. We were lucky to sell at the right time to the right people. It is interesting to note that several years later, I once again became an owner in Market Square, as I had invested in Bain Capital because of Mitt Romney, and then Bain Capital purchased Market Square along with the International Home Furnishings Center and several other buildings in High Point.

"Then, in 2017, the International Market Centers were purchased from Bain Capital by New-York-based private equity firm Blackstone. Bob Maricich, CEO of International Market Centers Inc., has done an incredible job assimilating these buildings in High Point, and they now constitute six-and-a-half million square feet of showroom space in High Point. His leadership is incredibly important to the future of High Point and our region."

Dave shared another personal story about Mack. Each year the Phillips family would take a family portrait for their Christmas card, continuing the tradition started by his parents. One year, the photography session was not going too smoothly. The family posed against the fence for that perfect Kodak moment, but it eluded them until Dave spotted the UPS man coming up the drive to the Phillips home.

Then the idea struck. Dave motioned for the UPS man to come over and join the Phillips family in the photo. "He had on his UPS outfit, his hat, his clipboard, and he looked just perfect. He was like a member of the family. We saw him practically every day. He came over and stood with us, and the picture was picture-perfect."

Mack was a member of the board of directors for UPS at the time, and after receiving the Phillips family Christmas card, he showed it at a board meeting. They all loved it, and the chairman of the board of directors at UPS wrote the Phillips family a letter that Dave gave to the driver who had appeared in the picture.

I learned that the sequence of Dave's three businesses merging or being sold over a very short period of time was very unusual. All three companies were sold within approximately a year's time. Not one of these business sales transactions were initiated by Dave. One simply led to another. Phillips Factors was sold to BB&T, Phillips Textiles was sold to Culp Inc., and Market Square was sold to Vornado. All three companies were listed on the New York Stock Exchange.

Dave remarked that he felt very lucky to be approached by these companies. I couldn't help but think Dave not only knew when to say no, but also knew when to say yes.

# CHAPTER 21

# *Rock House*

After the sales of Dave's businesses were finalized, Kay, Dave, and some friends embarked on a Mediterranean cruise. They were touring the island of Majorca, one of the Balearic Islands in the Mediterranean Sea, when Dave began to feel ill. His symptoms exacerbated to the point that he and Kay had to return to the States. He was admitted into the cardiac unit at Wake Forest University's Baptist Medical Center in Winston-Salem. The tests confirmed a blockage of the arteries, and stents were necessary. The following day, an angioplasty with stent placement was performed.

After recuperating from the surgery, Dave was again eager to travel. In August, almost three months after the heart operation, Kay, Dave, and their four daughters took a planned trip to India. After the first operation, the doctors had advised Dave that a condition called restenosis could occur, producing the same symptoms, but this would be very rare. Despite that, he was given the go-ahead to travel to India.

Among their stops was the city of Jodhpur, known as "Sun City" during summer and "Blue City" during the winter, where they enjoyed lunch with an elegant lady whose father had been the last Regent of India. The elderly lady showed Kay and Dave a painting of her father, Lieutenant-General His Highness Maharajadhiraja Maharaja Shri Sir Pratap Singh Sahib Bahadur of Idar, on the wall. An avid polo player, he was dressed in the customary polo outfit, including the highly recognizable Jodhpur riding pants. It was her father, the maharaja, who popularized these pants while playing polo. Designed by British tailors, they were billowy and then tapered tightly to the ankles, with leather patches on the inside leg for saddle protection. The pants were named for the city of Jodhpur, famous for championship polo teams.

Approximately ninety days after the first angioplasty, the pain suddenly struck once again, the same pain that Dave had experienced while in Majorca. However, luck was with him.

At the time of the reoccurrence, near the border of Pakistan, the Phillips family happened to be on the private plane of the chairman of the Oberoi Group, which owns Oberoi Hotels and Resorts, one of the most acclaimed hotel chains in the world. "Thank goodness we were on that plane because they made it possible to get back to the States quickly. I was back at Wake Forest Baptist Medical Center having another angioplasty with stent placement less than twenty-four hours later."

Still, it was unlike Dave just to relax; there was more to do following the sale of his businesses. Kay and Dave had always enjoyed going to the Blue Ridge Mountains of North Carolina. Through friends and old business partners George Lyles, Earl Slick, and Pat and John Bassett, they fell in love with the noted summer colony of Roaring Gap, with its magnificent mountain views, golf courses, and the amenities and friendships at the Roaring Gap Club. Dave described it as "tucked away in a cozy little spot of the Blue Ridge Mountains, perched three thousand feet above sea level and offering beautiful vistas." Roaring Gap has been known as a summer haven since 1890 when industrialist Alexander Chatham of Elkin, North Carolina, chose the area to build his summer home. Forty years after skeet shooting in Roaring Gap as a child, Dave rediscovered it again through his friends.

For several years, Kay and Dave rented homes at Roaring Gap. Dave was interested in buying a home there, but homes were rarely put on the real estate market. One particular home charmed both Dave and Kay. Earlier, Dave had called the owner, who lived in Florida, and asked if he was willing to sell it. The owner turned them down.

While Dave was recovering from his heart surgery, he decided to call the owner again. Fortunately, the owner and his wife changed their minds and sold their home to the Phillips.

The early homes built in the mountain retreat town in the early twentieth century were mostly wood-framed, weatherboard, or wood-shingled homes that featured wrap-around porches and verandas. The home purchased by the Phillips was built in 1926, a time when rustic architecture had become very popular for mountain living. Both Kay and Dave loved their mountain home and soon learned its history. Once they discovered its historic relevance, they restored it to its original condition.

"We discovered that the 'Rock House' had been built and designed for Bowman Gray, the president of R.J. Reynolds Company, by none other than Luther Lashmit, as I mentioned earlier," recalled Dave.

After restoration, the Rock House became the third property owned by Kay and Dave to be named on the National Register of Historic Places. I looked up the Rock House on the Register, and it was described as a "rambling, rock and chestnut-bark-clad design that emphasizes the use of native materials. The residence displays such hallmarks of Rustic Revival architecture, including massive stone chimneys and fireplaces, exposed timber trusses, and porches, decks, and terraces that afford magnificent sweeping views of the Yadkin River Valley. Gray's summer home survives among a collection of about a dozen other Rustic houses built in the picturesque environs of Roaring Gap."

On a clear day, the view from the Rock House is expansive. It is said that on such clear days, Gray would step onto the deck and look for the smoke billowing from the stack at R.J. Reynolds Company in Winston-Salem.

The picturesque view from the Rock House provided the perfect setting for a memorable milestone in Dave's life: his sixtieth birthday. Among the friends and family who helped celebrate Dave's birthday in 2002 was his former Choate headmaster Seymour St. John.

I learned that attending Choate (now Choate Rosemary Hall) had become a Phillips family tradition. All four of his daughters were accepted, and three attended, including his oldest daughter.

Like his father before him, when his oldest daughter graduated from Choate Rosemary Hall, Dave said, "I hope you are going to come back to the South to attend college." She Replied, "I want to come back to the South for college." Relieved, Dave added, "You will just love Chapel Hill." She said, "Dad, I want to go to Duke University." With that, she started a new Phillips family tradition of attending Duke University.

"I'll never forget when I took my oldest daughter to Duke for her interview," said Dave. "The admissions officer asked me point blank, 'Where did you go to college?'

"I sat there, surprised, and told him that I went to their archrival, Carolina."

"He probably didn't want to ask you any more questions after that!" I said, laughing.

Dave and Kay are clearly proud of their daughters and treasure the rare times when the family is together.

"My four daughters are just the most beautiful, phenomenal people. Of course, that's thanks to Kay.

"I'd love to brag on them, but they wouldn't like that," Dave admitted. "So, I'll just say that Kay and I have taken them to different countries and continents from the time they were very young. We taught them to go see the world—and they have. The spirit of adventure and travel has been transmitted to all four of them, which has been wonderful to see."

Dave and Kay's children truly have traveled broadly and enjoy diverse interests and talents. As a student at Duke University, their oldest daughter interned for director Joel Silver (*Lethal Weapon, The Matrix, Sherlock Holmes*) at Warner Brothers in Hollywood, California. After graduation, she moved to California and worked for the Creative Artists Agency (CAA) and for Davis Entertainment at Twentieth Century Fox, where she rose over the years to the position of vice president. After many years in the film business, she took a 180-degree turn and moved to New York City to work on Wall Street, passing the very difficult Series 7 and Series 63 tests required to be a licensed stock broker on her first try. She later obtained a degree in nutrition at Columbia University Teachers College while continuing her keen interest in private investments. According to Dave, she is also exploring the art world and has been invited by a prominent gallery for her first major showing in New York City.

Their second daughter also graduated from Choate Rosemary Hall and Duke University. With an interest in writing and publishing, she interned at W and In Style magazines, attended the famed Radcliffe Publishing Course in Boston, and after college worked for John F. Kennedy Jr. at George magazine in New York City. After a few years, she decided to change tack and move to San Francisco where she worked at the interior design firm Tucker and Marks. She then moved to London to obtain her degree in Fine and Decorative Arts at Christie's Education and master's degree in Historic Interiors and Decorative Arts at the Wallace Collection. Her one year in London became thirteen as she went on to study at Inchbald School of Design, work as an interior designer for Lady Spencer-Churchill's design firm, and complete interior design projects under her own business. She and her family currently live in Winston-Salem, North Carolina.

Their third daughter graduated from St. Catherine's in Richmond, Virginia, and then continued her sisters' tradition of attending Duke. After she got a taste of politics as a North Carolina page at the General Assembly, she continued her father's unique gift for crossing the political line. She worked for both Jesse Helms in Washington and Nancy Pelosi in San Francisco. After graduating from Duke University, she moved to New York City and studied cuisine at the French Culinary Institute and received her Grand Diplome in 2011. FCI then asked that she represent them in a special program at ALMA, the International School of Italian Cuisine where she studied under Massimo Buttura, one of the most renowned chefs in the world. Upon graduating at the top of her class, she continued her education in gastronomy at a Michelin-starred restaurant on Lake Como, Italy. She eventually returned to North Carolina, where she continues her ventures in gourmet specialty food.

Dave's youngest daughter graduated from Choate Rosemary Hall, but instead of attending Duke, she earned her BFA from Maryland Institute College of Art. She then moved to New York City and worked with renowned portrait artist, Aaron Shikler, whose portrait of Jacqueline Kennedy hangs in the White house. To widen her scope further, she also studied with classical realist painter Ben Long, known for his frescos in Italy and North Carolina. She most recently was a visiting artist at the American Academy in Rome and earned her MFA at the New York Academy of Art. She lives in New York City with her family.

As his daughters became involved in higher education, Dave did as well. He served on many educational boards, including the Duke Trinity Board of Trustees; Wake Forest University Graduate School of Business (chairman); Choate Rosemary Hall; Wake Forest University Medical Center; High Point University (vice-chairman); North Carolina School of the Arts Board of Visitors (chairman); and Westchester Academy Day School in High Point (chairman).

Being asked to serve on Choate's board of trustees is a moment Dave said he will never forget. "I had always gone back to Choate for reunions because I've always been grateful. One day, I got a call from the chairman of the board asking if I would serve on the board of trustees. I couldn't believe it. To get that call, after being such a screw-up the whole time I was at Choate—I was incredibly honored.

"I clearly remember my first board meeting, held at Mellon Library at eight thirty on a Saturday morning. I was sitting right next to Dr. St. John. He was no longer the headmaster but now served as a member of the board of trustees. I had seen him a few times in the previous twenty-five years, and I had always referred to him as Dr. St. John. The others in the room referred to him as Seymour. At lunch, others said I should refer to him as Seymour, too, and I did so after I returned to the meeting.

"I looked him in the eye and said, 'Seymour, did you ever think I would be sitting next to you at a board of trustees meeting at Choate?' He put his hand on my arm, looked me in the eye, and said, 'No, I really didn't.'"

Dave is very proud of his family's association with both Choate and Duke, and he wanted to support the schools further. Instead of simply giving money to a foundation or a building, he chose to do something more unique.

"I remembered hearing about a lecture series at another college that invited notable speakers and personalities. This particular college was small, but the lectures were major in scope.

"So, I proposed the idea of a lecture series to Choate, and they agreed. I also proposed it to Duke, and they too agreed. Since that time, both schools have brought in fabulous speakers. It's meant a lot to both institutions to have notable personalities talking to their students, and the students have benefited from it."

For example, at Duke, Kay and Dave's endowment for the Phillips Family International Lecture Series has brought in speakers such as Robert Gates, former US secretary of defense; Condoleezza Rice, US secretary of state under President Bush; Karl Rove and Howard Dean, together on stage; General David Petraeus, former director of the CIA; and Governor Mitt Romney.

It was hoped that Russian President Vladimir Putin would be a speaker for the Duke Lecture Series, and because of Dave's relationship with Russian ambassador to Estonia, Nikolay Uspensky, it almost happened. The president of Duke University wrote an invitation that was approved by the US State Department and sent to Putin, but he did not accept.

# CHAPTER 22

# *Jupiter Island*

Through the years, the Phillips family had also enjoyed spending the winter holidays on Jupiter Island, Florida. In fact, it wasn't long after the sale of his companies and time spent in state government that Dave and his family first discovered the island's mystique.

Small and intimate, Jupiter Island is located at the southernmost of Florida's three Barrier Islands, directly north of West Palm Beach. The island's history is rich with lore dating back to 1715 when the Spanish Plate Fleet wrecked off the coast, leaving gold and silver coins in its wake. According to the historians, the story of Jupiter Island began as a development of natural land and continues as a story of ongoing respect and careful preservation of that land.

Dave told me there were so many stories that could be told about Jupiter Island, especially since the Jupiter Island Club was founded in the 1930s by the mining and oil heiress Permelia Reed. "No drunks, no party-pushers, no rudeness to the employees," she once said. She was quite a character and, according to her son Nathaniel Pryor Reed, did nothing to dispute the story that she would send any member who broke the rules a black sweater that was synonymous with an exit visa. Since Permelia's death in 1994, the Jupiter Island Club has been owned by its members.

Both Kay and Dave loved going to Jupiter Island and especially as guests of Pat and John Bassett, who had also introduced them to the mountain club in Roaring Gap. The Bassett family had long enjoyed the solitude and fishing on the island, well before the private club was formed. There is even a creek called Bassett Creek.

"So, here was a surprise," Dave told me. "During one of the first times we went down to Jupiter Island to visit the Bassetts, they took us to church, and when I came out of church, I saw Seymour St. John standing there in his robe. He was the minister of the church! I think he was as stunned to see me as I was to see him."

It turned out Seymour St. John also had a home on Jupiter Island. The St. John family bought and developed land on Jupiter Island in the 1920s or '30s—also before the private club was established. There was great fishing there, and father and son loved to fish.

Dave and St. John's once tumultuous relationship would, in later life, turn into a deep and esteemed friendship. The same headmaster who suspended Dave from Choate would support Dave and Kay's membership in the Jupiter Island Club.

St. John and Dave would often reminisce about the days at Choate. "He was the stern headmaster and remembered that I got into a lot of trouble and that he had to discipline me. I didn't appreciate it at the time, but if it weren't for Seymour, I would have never graduated from Choate. I am forever grateful to him. He changed my life."

At Choate, Seymour had impacted Dave's life much more deeply than just teaching him basic educational skills. Seymour's commitment to education extended far beyond the classroom and far beyond the meadows at Choate. He had impacted Dave's character and fostered a worldwide consciousness in the spirited young boy, who would carry these lessons for a lifetime.

Kay and Dave had rented a home on Jupiter Island, so one weekend Dave traveled to Jupiter Island to begin the lease that was signed and paid for the year before. Kay had to stay in High Point to tend to her two female Himalayan bears that were undergoing hysterectomies. The veterinarians of the Veterinary School at North Carolina State University were performing the operations for both Jane and Isabella. Kay wanted the hysterectomies because even "female bears have bad days."

Admittedly, neither Kay nor Dave ever saw or sensed that the bears ever had a bad day but were fortunate to get the veterinarians to operate. Dave noted that Kay's love for her animals is reciprocated. "Although they weigh 350 pounds each, she can hug the bears when no one else can. The bears are vegetarians, and they have never tasted meat. They are docile, but they still have their teeth and claws. However, she has always shown great respect to them and is very careful," added Dave. This was a rare opportunity for the veterinarians from North Carolina State University.

Five veterinarians came to Valleyfields Farm, several out of curiosity, because it was a very unusual situation. Kay encouraged Dave to go on to Jupiter Island without her since "you can't do anything for the bears." She would join him a few days later.

Dave arrived at their rental home. He had been there little more than a day when the realtor stopped by. She told Dave that there was a house just up the street that was going to be put on the market on Monday. She thought that Kay and Dave would appreciate the old home, even though it needed some major repairs. Dave could immediately see the potential of the home but wanted Kay to see it before making any decision.

Timing became of the essence, and Dave asked the owner to please wait a few days until Kay arrived and could see it. The owner agreed. They did indeed buy the home; the story would get even more interesting as the history of the home was revealed.

As soon as the papers were signed, the neighbors started telling Kay and Dave about the historical significance of the home they had just purchased. The *Palm Beach Post* wrote an article with the headline, "Peculiar History May Save a Home Inhabited by Stars." The article described the home, built around the turn of the twentieth century, as "hidden by a dark, tropical jungle and laced with spiral staircases and secret passageways—the mysterious, fairy-tale kind of place that inspires tall tales and shameless lies."

The neighbors said, "Do you know who some of the previous owners were?" Kay and Dave answered no. The home, known as Gate House, is not just one home but four different small buildings connected together, all in the Mediterranean style of off-white stucco and red roof tiles.

It is said that the house got its name from the words "Gate House" etched in the tile on one of the out buildings, which may have once been the entryway to the property. One of the cottages on the property is called the Donkey House because it was a stable for the donkeys that were owned by neighbor Edsel Ford.

The story goes that Ford built a dock on the adjacent property to moor his large yacht. It is said that Ford took friends around the island on his donkey carts and stabled the animals in the Donkey House, now used as a dining room by the Phillips.

An amazing story concerning Gate House comes from the noted playwright Philip Barry and his wife. Barry wrote *The Philadelphia Story*, his most famous play, on the third floor of Gate House, according to island historian Vee Chambers, who was his secretary at the time. It was Chambers who transcribed the play from the yellow legal pad. It was said, albeit not by Chambers, that Barry preferred writing outdoors on the front porch, half-naked while drinking whiskey.

One of the most interesting stories concerning Gate House involves two of Barry's close friends, Spencer Tracy and Katharine Hepburn. Hepburn starred in the stage play and the movie version of *The Philadelphia Story*. The rumor mill reported that Gate House provided the perfect getaway for a Tracy-Hepburn affair, away from the paparazzi and gossip columnists of Hollywood. Even though they rented a house together in West Hollywood during their twenty-six years together, their affair was perceived as semi-secret, a secret everyone knew. Tracy was separated from his wife, but as a Catholic, his wife did not believe in divorce.

The next interesting owner was John Walker III, the director of the National Gallery in Washington, DC, until his retirement in 1969; he lived at Gate House until his death in 1995.

With its unique Mediterranean architecture and interesting history, Kay and Dave decided not only to renovate Gate House but to restore it to its original structure. In doing so, Gate House would be listed in the National Register of

Historic Places. This would be the fourth such designation for the Phillips, the first being Market Square, the second the Moore Cabin on Valleyfields Farm, and the third the Rock House in Roaring Gap. Today, Gate House remains the only building on Jupiter Island to be listed on the National Register of Historic Places.

Throughout their married life, Kay and Dave have recognized the importance of historic preservation, both in their home state of North Carolina and in Florida. Yet it takes dedication and commitment: there are codes to be met, and the restoration process for a home or a building is time-consuming, involving extensive research. The end result is much like an open book, preserving stories upon stories of previous owners, memories of historic times, and a new lifetime ahead.

Before buying their Jupiter Island home, Kay and Dave had rented several homes on the island. One of those was the home of General Joseph A. McChristian, who served as the US Army assistant chief of staff for intelligence under General George S. Patton and as the assistant chief of staff for intelligence under General William Westmoreland.

With the purchase of Gate House and now under consideration for membership at the Jupiter Island Club, Kay and Dave couldn't help but remember this former landlord and "the story of the bears."

General McChristian was known as an old-school, tough army man. He sported a crewcut and postured an imposing stance. The realtor who handled the rental had informed Kay and Dave that the general had specific rules of "no pets."

However, when Kay got her second Himalayan bear, it was just a cub about to open her eyes. Kay wanted to imprint her smell on the bear for safety and didn't want to leave her in High Point. "I can't go to Florida without the bear," she told Dave. "Our rental contract states that we can't even have a parakeet," Dave countered; however, Kay brought the bear cub to Florida anyway. The cub was small enough to carry in a papoose, and it sat on her lap on the plane.

Word quickly went around the neighborhood that there was a bear in General McChristian's home. At night, the cub stayed in a dog kennel in the kitchen that Pat Bassett had loaned them. Nevertheless, the secret was about to be exposed when the realtor stopped by the home.

Dave said that he was really worried when the realtor was about to go into the kitchen to replace the coffee pot. The minutes were ticking down to when the bear caper would be uncovered, so Dave finally confessed, "I have something to tell you. I know we aren't supposed to have any animals, but Kay brought her pet bear cub. The bear won't be any problem. It's not like a dog chewing up the furniture." Dave thought the realtor was going to faint. He took her into the kitchen to see the little bear cub, and she agreed that the cub was the cutest thing she had ever seen, but she did warn Dave, "We cannot let the general know about this."

Now that they were residents of Jupiter Island, Dave, cognizant of the high standards that were expected of members of the Jupiter Island Club, became a bit nervous. Dave told Kay, "They will think we are crazy, and they will never let us into the club." Kay and Dave certainly didn't want to receive the proverbial black sweater, even if it was cashmere. Would Kay and Dave survive the great bear escapade?

The bear remained a not-so-well-kept secret for about a year. After they were accepted into the club, Kay and Dave were at a cocktail party when General McChristian approached and said, "I just have to ask you something that has been bothering me. I heard that you had a bear in my house, but I know that couldn't possibly be true, could it?" Dave said, "Yes, General, that is true." General McChristian answered, "Well, damn! I wish I could have seen that!"

# CHAPTER 23

# *The Dalai Lama*

I n addition to Roaring Gap and Jupiter Island, Kay and Dave often visited friends and family in California, including Lil in Los Angeles and Kate in San Francisco. Dave had also attended California's furniture markets over the years, also held in those cities, which were the original inspiration for Market Square. During his travels to California, Dave got to know many people, which led to the invitation to join the private Bohemian Club in San Francisco and to become an investor in Pebble Beach in Monterey.

At Pebble Beach, Dave enjoyed playing golf with his friend Paul Stephens, whom he had met when their children attended Duke University together. Dave and Stephens's friendship provided a once-in-a-lifetime experience that transpired when Dave visited Stephens at his home in Hawaii.

Stephens's home, located on Hawaii's Big Island, had a beautiful view overlooking the Pacific Ocean. They played golf at the Nanea Golf Club, one of the most unusual private golf courses in the world, located on the side of a volcanic crater. In the evening, the Stephens hosted a birthday party for Jeanne Robertson, the wife of Stephens's former business partner, Sanford (Sandy) Robertson.

While Dave was sitting next to Jeanne at the mountainside birthday party, the conversation took an interesting twist. She had just returned from India and had visited with the Dalai Lama.

Meeting Jeanne was opportune as Dave was able to describe the trip he was planning for the National Board of Trustees of the Smithsonian Institution.

Earlier, Dave had been asked to serve on the Smithsonian National Board of Trustees by his friend Frank Daniels, chairman of Associated Press and owner of the *Raleigh News and Observer*, and who also happened to be chairman of the Smithsonian board.

As an aside, Dave shared an interesting anecdote: During one of the board meetings, Dave posed the question of how to educate the public on the institution's artifacts, which number over 155 million. He had often watched the National Geographic Channel, and it struck him that a Smithsonian TV channel could tell even more stories. The Smithsonian Channel would debut on September 26, 2007.

Each year, it had been customary for the board of trustees to travel to a different part of the world that would have a special meaning and afford a great experience for the members who hailed from all over the United States. As chairman of the travel committee, Dave proposed that they travel to India; they agreed that the experience would be fascinating.

Dave embraced the challenge and began formulating an itinerary. He thought of the places in India where his family had visited. Kay suggested that meeting the Dalai Lama, the exiled political and spiritual leader of Tibet, would be a monumental experience. Monumental, yes, but probable, no! The logistics of a trip to India with the Smithsonian Institution Board of Trustees needed to be well planned.

Dave's arrangements for the Smithsonian trip to India had to be made outside of normal governmental channels. Neither the offices of the Smithsonian nor the government contacts could be used to arrange for an audience with the Dalai Lama. United States relations with China were strained, and since the Dalai Lama had been exiled from Tibet, an autonomous province of the People's Republic of China, these arrangements could offend the Chinese. If

Dave made travel arrangements for this meeting through a government channel, both governments would have taken a dim view.

The good fortune to have been seated next to Jeanne Robertson was incalculable. As she spoke, Dave listened intently and then asked, "How did you do it?" She offered her assistance, and Dave followed up immediately. The US government knew of Dave's intent to take the Smithsonian board of trustees to have an audience with the Dalai Lama. Since the board members who would be taking the trip were private citizens and not government officials, there was no opposition from the government.

Excitement built as the trip neared. The group chartered small planes for the trip to Northern India. They landed at the Gaggal Airport, about an hour away from the mountainous terrain of Dharamshala, the center of the Tibetan government in exile and also a Buddhist pilgrimage center. After arriving at Dharamshala, they traversed farther up the mountain to the village of McLeod Ganj, the home of the exiled Dalai Lama, whose religious name is Tenzin Gyatso.

The group approached a small, unpretentious white stucco house, formerly a British hill station, amidst a dense forest. It stood just one story high and seemed more like a mountain cottage, in contrast to the palatial palace that was the Dalai Lama's home in Tibet before he was exiled. The group wondered, could this really be the home of the Dalai Lama? They looked around their sparsely and simply furnished surroundings in amazement. The modest home did, however, have spectacular views of the snow-capped peaks of the Himalayans.

The members of the group were also somewhat astonished at the visible lack of security. Concerned, they posed the question of security for the Dalai Lama, and they were assured that there was security for his safety. Dave said, "We weren't concerned about our own safety, but we were worried about the Dalai Lama. There had been a lot of trouble in Northern India at the time." After all, he was in exile, and he was known throughout the world as the spiritual leader of the Buddhists. But then, perhaps, this simplicity of living paralleled his ideology of religion: "This is my simple religion. There is no need for temples; no need for complicated philosophy. Our own brain, our own heart is our temple; the philosophy is kindness."

As they waited for the Dalai Lama, they saw many monks in saffron robes who were on a special retreat. One monk instructed the Smithsonian group on the correct way to greet the Dalai Lama for their private audience. Social etiquette states that the encounter will be brief. One must bow his or her head to greet him, and eye contact is not advised. They were also instructed on how to pose their hands when bowing.

The group was prepared for the reverence of the momentous occasion as they solemnly awaited his entrance. They expected a very pious Dalai Lama to arrive, assuming a venerable godliness. All of a sudden, the Dalai Lama appeared.

Dave recalled, "Since I was to make the presentation, I was told how to do it. I was nervous. I was told how to hold my hands and how to present myself to him. The Dalai Lama came in with a big grin on his face. Before I could do anything, he stuck out his hand and said, 'Hey, how are you doing?' We all started laughing. There is a picture of me with this incredulous look on my face."

The group from the Smithsonian brought a token of appreciation as a gift for the holy leader. The Dalai Lama had traveled to Washington, DC, following the tragic events of September 11, 2001, to give comfort and bestow his blessings upon America. At that time, he also visited the Smithsonian Institution. Dave presented him with a mounted photograph of his visit to the Smithsonian and a plaque of recognition thanking him for what he had done for America. Dave describes the Dalai Lama as "comforting and gracious" as they talked.

After some time, a young man entered the room. He was not wearing a saffron robe; instead, he wore a wrap around his waist and a shirt with a button-down collar. He was introduced as a family member. Dave recalled, "We started talking about worldly matters when the nephew leaned over to me and said, 'March Madness,' and although it was the month of March, I was confused and said to him, 'Are you talking about the madness in the world?' He said, 'No, I'm talking about March Madness basketball. I understand you're from North Carolina. I went to Georgetown.' We all started laughing. He wanted to talk about basketball. So, here we are with the religious leader the Dalai Lama, high up in the Himalayas, and we are talking about basketball. It was unbelievable."

After the conversation ended, the Dalai Lama presented a white ceremonial prayer scarf known as a khata (signifying purity and compassion) to each person.

As he put it around each person's neck, he gave a short blessing, but something more ethereal happened as he placed the white shawl on Kay's neck. The Dalai Lama put Kay's face in his hands and looked into her eyes. There was such a spirituality about it; the group felt a wondrous aura as they watched her spirit seemingly transcend across the Himalayas. A mystifying and metaphysical spirituality radiated through the mountain retreat. "It was all very magical and just one of those moments for all of us, especially Kay."

Other travels in India included the holy city of Varanasi located on the Ganges River, the "River to Heaven." It is the cherished aspiration of the Hindu faithful to be cremated there as it assures the washing away of all sins and the liberation from the cycle of earthly life.

The Smithsonian group was astonished to see corpses wrapped in cloth on the tops of cars as families traveled to bring their deceased loved ones to scatter their ashes in the "River to Heaven." They had been told of this religious custom but were still in awe as they witnessed the pyres of bodies on the banks of the Ganges River. "It was beautiful and ceremonial as the families cremated their loved ones."

After the highlights of the private meeting with the Dalai Lama and the witnessing of the holy cremation services, the National Board of Trustees visited the Khajuraho Group of Monuments located in the small town of Khajuraho in the Indian state of Madhya Pradesh. This is one of the most frequented and popular tourist attractions in India, known for the medieval Hindu and Jain temples featuring erotic sculptures, interpreted as the basis of the Kama Sutra philosophy on human sexual behavior.

The deep impact of meeting with the Dalai Lama would remain with Kay and Dave and other members of the Smithsonian team for the rest of their lives.

Later that evening, I found myself reflecting on Dave's once-in-a-lifetime experiences and how they seemed to unfold so effortlessly. It all seemed to come down to relationships. If you truly enjoy people and have the confidence to walk through the doors that open for you, you can't help but find success.

# CHAPTER 24

# The Road to the Embassy

Although Dave had been involved in the political arena for several decades, he had not been involved in George W. Bush's campaign in 1999 because of his three-year commitment to the Special Olympics.

Dave remembered meeting President Bush for the first time at the Lawrence Joel Veterans Memorial Coliseum in Winston-Salem, North Carolina, in 2002, when he was introduced to Bush by Senator Helms. President Bush approached Dave to take a leadership role in his reelection campaign. "I agreed to work for Bush's reelection and was honored to do so. Kay and I took our family to the Republican National Convention in 2004. It was a great experience."

Kay and Dave became friends with Bush in North Carolina, a friendship that grew with future get-togethers at the Bush ranch in Texas and the family compound in Kennebunkport, Maine.

The road to Estonia emerged one day when Dave was at the Bohemian Club in San Francisco. He received a phone call from Karl Rove.

"He said, 'The president would like to nominate you as ambassador to Estonia.'"

Dave was very excited to be asked but decided to wait until he returned home to North Carolina from California to discuss the idea with Kay. "Kay knew that something was up the minute I walked in the door," said Dave.

Kay thought it would be great, and Dave accepted the appointment from the president.

Saying yes was only the beginning of the process. After the vetting, both Kay and Dave were then required to attend the diplomat's version of "charm school" for three months in 2007 before appearing before the Senate Foreign Relations Committee. Every day, they, along with other appointees, were schooled in all areas of the US government. The fellow diplomats were going to various parts of the world, including Belgium, Saudi Arabia, Poland, the Dominican Republic, Estonia, and Swaziland in Southern Africa.

Dave remembered an intriguing offer made to them by the diplomat going to Swaziland. Each year at the Umhlanga (Reed Dance) Festival, the king—the current king's father had seventy wives—has the option of choosing a new wife from the many bare-chested virgins who dance before him in hopes of becoming the newest bride. If the king planned to select another wife at the upcoming festival, the diplomat said he would invite the Phillips down to the festival.

Regrettably, Dave said, the invitation to the Umhlanga Festival from the Swaziland ambassador did not materialize.

The three-month schedule at charm school was rigorous. "Kay and I did our homework every night. It was intense, and we were there with career diplomats who already had government experience."

All of this was in preparation for Dave to go before the Senate Foreign Relations Committee for approval to confirm his appointment. Finally, he was informed that the date had been set for shortly before Easter. At that time, Barack Obama was the US senator for the state of Illinois and served as the acting chairman of the Foreign Relations Committee, standing in for Senator Biden.

During a protocol presentation in charm school, Kay and Dave learned that as a US ambassador, he would be referred to as "Your Excellency." Kay was very amused at this new designation for her husband and quickly posed the question to the government official, "How do I introduce him?" To that the advisor asked, "What do you call him at home?" Her response was quick: "At home, I call him a—hole." That unexpected response drew howls from the charm school "students."

The Senate hearing for the ambassadorial appointment of Dave was considered to be non-controversial. The Phillips family, including Kay and three of their daughters attended the hearing. Their second daughter was unable to come from London for the occasion.

Dave was well prepared. For days prior to the actual hearings, the State Department had grilled Dave on any possible questions the committee might pose.

The time had finally arrived, and the family entered the Senate Hearing Room. The ornate Foreign Relations Room was full. Another appointee was also up for approval for a US ambassador assignment: Sam Fox, a St. Louis businessman who had been nominated as ambassador to Belgium. Senator Kerry would pose a major obstacle in the hearing opposing the appointment of Dave's counterpart.

Fox was more than just a controversial diplomatic candidate for Kerry; he was his adversary. Fox was credited for helping defeat Kerry in the presidential campaign.

The hearing needed just one senator to vote against Fox to prevent his appointment. Fox brought advocates for his nomination, a large number of family members and supporters.

The Phillips family, thankful they were not in the center of the potential minefield, waited calmly amidst the tension that permeated the air. Chairman Obama got out of his seat and walked over to the Phillips family and greeted them warmly. "My family thought it was a very gracious gesture," said Dave.

On either side of the family were North Carolina senators Elizabeth Dole and Richard Burr, who were presenting Dave. Then the hearings began. "At the beginning, most of the questions were mostly directed at me and none to Sam, but that was soon to change," Dave recalled.

"It was just like a trial. Kerry said to Fox, 'I have been watching your testimony in my office, and I have a lot of questions for you.' Kerry's focus on Sam was unnerving to everyone. Kerry used to be a prosecutor in the District

Attorney's Office in Boston, so it was not a friendly situation. However, it took the heat off of me, and I was confirmed by the full Senate in a couple of days."

Fox's appointment was not confirmed, but that would not end his quest. Ultimately, it resulted in yet another controversy. With such opposition to the confirmation of his appointment of Fox, Bush withdrew the nomination. This action appeased the Democrats temporarily, but that was not the end of the story and definitely not the end of the controversy.

The president used his power of a recess appointment to confirm Fox and to override the Senate. Recess appointments are permitted in the Constitution of the United States, but they have regularly caused contention between the president and the Senate since the beginning of the nation.

The Senate Democrats responded quickly and demanded the Government Accountability Office make a full investigation.

Fortunately, no such controversy existed with Dave's appointment, and he was sworn in as US ambassador to Estonia by Condoleezza Rice on April 16, 2007, at a ceremony at the State Department in Washington, DC. As Rice was introducing Dave at the swearing-in ceremony, she referred to his historic trip to Russia as a teenager: "As a high school student in 1961, he participated in one of the first student exchange programs between the United States and the Soviet Union, attending Moscow State University. He travelled extensively though Russia, Ukraine, Georgia, and Poland." Rice also noted that it was unusual for a diplomat, especially a political appointee from the business community rather than a career diplomat, to have this type of travel experience behind the Iron Curtain.

Thus, Dave became the sixth US ambassador to Estonia since the country gained its independence in 1991.

# CHAPTER 25

# US Ambassador to Estonia

S oon the Phillips prepared for their move to Estonia. They were excited and looked forward to their new adventure and the new culture. Kay had two major requests for the trip. She could not go without her pets, at least her indoor pets. The bison, bears, llamas, camel, and zebra would all have to remain in North Carolina. However, their dog Helen, their cat Permelia (after Jupiter Island's Permelia Reed), and Oliver the ferret would all travel to Estonia with the Phillips.

The second request was more unusual and always garners more than a chuckle when told. Kay's favorite libation is bourbon. Did Estonia have bourbon? Now, Benjamin Franklin said, "When in doubt, don't," but in Kay Phillips's perspective, "When in doubt, do." So, in addition to the dog, the cat, and the ferret, seventeen cases of bourbon accompanied the Phillips on their plane to Estonia. Dave added that when they moved into the residence, the dog food, the ferret food, the cat food, and the bourbon were all kept in the highly secure safe room. Kay wanted to be sure she could feed her animals if there was a problem.

The State Department had briefed the Phillips, just the day before, that there were "serious frustrations" in Estonia at the time the Phillips were scheduled to arrive.

Approximately one-fourth of the population of Estonia is ethnic Russian, dating back to the occupation of Estonia by the Russians in 1940. Unrest had broken out after the Estonian government removed the Bronze Soldier Statue from Freedom Square in downtown Tallinn. The statue was viewed as a tribute to Red Army soldiers who died fighting the Nazis; however, many native Estonians viewed the Bronze Soldier as a painful reminder of hardships under Soviet rule. The Bronze Soldier depicts a Red Army soldier in uniform, his helmet in one hand, his head slightly bowed, and his rifle slung over his back.

Kay and Dave were unaware of the gravity of the situation as they arrived at Lennart Meri Tallinn Airport. A security team from the American Embassy waited to pick up the Phillips. After loading everything into the vehicles, Kay had a request of the driver and asked if, before going to their residence, they could just drive through Old Town, the cobblestoned medieval area of Tallinn, recognized as a United Nations World Heritage site.

"No ma'am, you can't; there is a disturbance going on downtown. We will have to bypass and go to your home on the other side of town," answered the driver. Kay and Dave questioned just what kind of "disturbance" this was. At that point, the security officer turned to Kay and said, "Ma'am, in America, we call it a riot."

The "riot" turned out to be the worst that Estonia had seen in the sixteen years since gaining independence from Russia. As the Molotov cocktails flew on the streets, a wave of digital violence hit Estonia that caught the country completely off-guard.

"Here we were, right in the middle of it," Dave commented, recalling the cyberattack. "Estonia was the first sovereign nation in the world that had been attacked via cyber warfare. That began our incredible journey in Estonia. My job became intense because the US government became actively involved in dealing with the situation."

Within a short period of time, cyber experts arrived to support Estonia. US Secretary of Homeland Security Michael Chertoff arrived later, as did House

Majority Leader John Boehner, and then Secretary of Defense Robert Gates. Later, Secretary Gates would dedicate the NATO Cooperative Cyber Defence Centre of Excellence in Estonia.

In an interview for the *Postimees* daily newspaper, just two weeks after Kay and Dave's arrival in Estonia, Dave commented, "Since I arrived here two weeks ago, I feel like I am a part of history. This is what the Bronze Soldier is all about—a symbol of history. It is something that involves many emotions."

The Bronze Soldier was moved to the Tallinn Military Cemetery. The diplomatic corps invited Dave to attend, even though he had not yet had the chance to present his credentials to the Estonian president. He had not even met any of the other ambassadors. When he was told to stand near the statue of the Bronze Soldier, he felt a sense of pride. He didn't know until the next morning that standing near the Bronze Soldier was a dangerous position, and some of those around him had donned bulletproof vests. "I was the new kid on the block," Dave says of the incident. "Fortunately, it was a peaceful ceremony."

He continued, "Their nation was being shut down using cyber warfare. They couldn't use their normal facilities. It was a ripple effect from the capital city, and the country itself became an immense problem. There were all sorts of rumors as to what would happen next . . . an invasion? Just a year later, the Russian forces did invade Georgia, which was preceded by a cyberattack. Many Estonians felt that an invasion was imminent."

The cyberattacks were targeted at gaining access to Estonia's information infrastructure. At first, they began with a denial-of-service (DOS) that crippled the site of Estonia's prime minister and the nation's largest banks. The ramifications of the cyberattacks were substantial. Estonia is known as one of the world's most technologically advanced countries, making them digitally dependent. The capital of Estonia, Tallinn, has been selected for many years as one of the world's most intelligent cities. Tallinn is also the birthplace of Skype, described as "calling, seeing, messaging, and sharing with others wherever they are." A cyberattack on Estonia could cause a critical governmental breakdown.

Ene Ergma, the Speaker of the Estonian parliament, made the astute comment, "Like nuclear radiation, cyberwar doesn't make you bleed, but it can destroy everything." The attack blocked websites and paralyzed the country's entire internet infrastructure. At the pinnacle of the attacks, bankcards and cell phone networks were frozen, setting off alarms. This was significant to Estonia, a country who relied on high-tech, computerized infrastructure and had created a paperless society, giving Estonia the reputation as the most wired country in Europe. Russia was the prime suspect. The disclosures made by Edward Snowden in the WikiLeaks documents, later documented by the Estonian press, confirmed it was, indeed, Russia responsible for the cyberwar with Estonia.

"The [government of Estonia] believes it has enough circumstantial evidence to link Moscow with the attacks," the cable stated, citing a conversation between Estonia's president, Toomas Hendrik Ilves, and the US ambassador at the time, S. Davis Phillips. A certain government official continued to pose the question, "Who benefits from these attacks?" and speculated that these cyberattacks fit the modus operandi of Vladimir Putin's testing of a "new weapon."

"I remember the first press conference when the Estonians felt a Russian invasion was imminent. They were asking me, 'What will America do? Will America support Estonia?' The position was, and still is, that America would support Estonia because of Article 5 of the North Atlantic Trade Organization (NATO), which provides that if a NATO ally is a victim of armed attack, each and every other member of the alliance will consider this an act of violence against all members. The United States and Estonia are important allies and partners." Dave added, "It was one of those incredible situations that you are talking about an invasion, and here we are right in the middle of it from day one."

The US Embassy in Tallinn is an old-world limestone building, first used as the US Embassy in the 1920s and '30s, up until the Soviet invasion in 1938. According to Dave, the former embassy building was the obvious venue to reopen the old embassy. It was not a glamorous embassy, and the United States originally shared the location with the British. With ninety employees at the US Embassy alone, the space was rather tight. Dave acknowledged that security was strong, and "you felt secure." The Embassy was located just a few blocks from the walled, medieval Old Town, dating back to the thirteenth century. The tourist attraction is known for its gothic spires, cobblestone streets, markets, and ancient architecture while also offering Wi-Fi and cappuccino shops.

In contrast to the crowded quarters at the US Embassy in Tallinn, the ambassador's home was just outside of Tallinn in the town of Pirita, overlooking the Baltic Sea. Also in contrast to the Embassy and nearby Old Town, the residence was ultra-modern. Ironically, the Estonian residence was owned by a Russian. The Russian had purchased the land in Estonia after it gained its independence in 1991. As part of the new wave of capitalistic Russians, he bought the land as an investment for a development to build luxurious homes.

According to Dave, "It was very large and very comfortable. There was a lot of land around it. The yard was fenced in with several guard gates and guard posts. It was secure but open and airy. They had a wonderful indoor heated swimming pool that was a treat for us. The indoor swimming pool in the house overlooking the Baltic was enticing, especially during those long, cold winters of snow and ice. This was a welcome relief, and we enjoyed the home very much."

The home also provided a wonderful venue for Kay to continue her passionate involvement in the arts. As a former board member of the Art Society of the North Carolina Museum of Art, Kay was able to borrow thirty-two pieces of art from the museum for their spacious Estonian residence.

"I do want to clarify that Kay and I paid for the freight and insurance on these paintings, not the taxpayers," Dave added.

"The Estonians were very impressed with the art collection from North Carolina. It was great exposure for our state and a wonderful addition to the US Embassy residence."

The unprecedented art exhibit heightened the Estonians' and visiting dignitaries' cultural awareness of North Carolina. One journalist, Dmitriy Babichenko, was among those invited to see the paintings. Along with many Estonian cultural personalities, he was impressed with the gracious hospitality of the Phillips, and wrote, "A couple of days ago, US ambassador to Estonia, Dave Phillips, and his wife, Kay, invited Estonian cultural figures and journalists to their home to show them a superb collection from their home state of North Carolina that adorns the walls of the residence."

The art collection garnered even more interest since the Kumu Art Museum in Tallinn had just opened in 2006. Kumu serves as the headquarters for the Art Museum of Estonia, displaying both Estonian art classics and modern designs.

During the time that Kay and Dave were in Estonia, the Kumu Art Museum was recognized as the best new museum in Europe and was the winner of the European Museum of the Year Award.

"What was it like living in Estonia?" I asked.

"There were many functions in all the embassies, so you got to know all the different ambassadors. For example, we met the Chinese ambassador, and Kay let her know that we had Chinese food every Sunday night in America. So, she would invite us over to the Chinese Embassy to have Chinese food on Sunday night.

"Kay was especially known for her July Fourth celebrations. Marines would march, and the music would play.

"But instead of everybody just sipping a little wine and saying hello, Kay mixed it up a bit with all kinds of different drinks from America. You could go to one bar and get a margarita and go to another and get Long Island Iced Tea.

"They had no idea what they were drinking, so you can just imagine all the dignitaries at these parties . . . Well, that's all I'm going to say about that," Dave finished, laughing.

# CHAPTER 26

# A Small World

Of the many relationships Dave forged in Estonia, none was more significant than with the ambassador of the Russian Federation to Estonia, Nikolai Uspenski. This was particularly notable since their meeting directly correlated to the timetable of the presumed Russian cyberattack.

"Nikolai and I met in the worst of times, dealing with the riots and the cyberattack. Fortunately, he spoke perfect English. He was known as The Interpreter, since he had been the interpreter for Mikhail Gorbachev (general secretary of the Communist Party of the Soviet Union) during the Reykjavik Summit in Iceland with President Reagan in 1986. Nikolai had also lived in Washington and worked at the Russian Embassy. He was intrigued that I had visited Russia as a teenager.

"Because of the tense situation between Estonia and Russia, we were forced together, yet we became friendly. Nikolai's wife, Larissa, and Kay also became friendly. I can visualize the night the four of us went to the performance by the acclaimed Russian Bolshoi Ballet at the Estonia Concert Hall. We walked into the concert hall together, and you could just feel the tension in the room because, at the time, about one-fourth of the population in Estonia was Russian expatriates who had remained after the occupation of Estonia. So, for us to walk in and sit down and watch the ballet together sent a very strong and calming message to both the Russians and the Estonians.

"My relationship with the Russian ambassador was part of my job. It fit into the philosophy of knowing your opposition," said Dave.

The relationship between the ambassadors extended to their families. One Thanksgiving Day spent in Moscow, Kay and Dave invited Uspenski's daughter and her fiancé to join the Phillips family for dinner. Dave recalled dining at the very fanciful restaurant, Pushkin. "I'll never forget the conversation. She asked us, 'What is Thanksgiving?'" The Phillips were happy to share its cultural and historical meaning.

Normal diplomatic protocol suggests that upon the arrival of a US ambassador in his assigned country, the newly designated ambassador presents his credentials to the head of the foreign country. This formal ceremony marks the official recognition of the foreign ambassador. On May 31, 2007, Dave presented his credentials to the Estonian president, Toomas Hendrik Ilves. He remembers the ceremonial walk on the red carpet to make the presentation to the Estonian president at the presidential office, with Kay and his four daughters present.

The secretary of protocol made the walk with him, just to the side of the red carpet. All eyes were on the US ambassador as the flags of both countries were raised and the anthems were played. Estonian soldiers and the Estonian band lined the red carpet as Dave made his way toward the president.

"My greatest fear was that I would stumble and my leg would fall off," Dave admitted. The fear stemmed from the uneven stones beneath the carpet laid especially for this grand occasion. "There is an attachment clip on my leg that could unclip if I hit bumps in a wrong way. It had happened before. I was looking straight ahead, just hoping I wouldn't embarrass America, my family, or myself."

The official photograph of Dave on the red carpet shows a very intense, serious man. While the ceremony was formal and very dignified, this intensity was not characteristic of the affable Dave. That "twinkle" and smile returned just at the thought of his "leg" lying on the red carpet during such a ceremonious and dignified occasion. Fortunately, that did not happen, and Dave made the presentation of his credentials to the president of Estonia.

As the tensions eased and the credentials had been presented, Kay and Dave were able to enjoy the culture and the people of Estonia. Periodically, Dave attended meetings in Europe. Sometimes the travel plans were rather unpredictable, due to scheduling and connection difficulties. There was one such instance that amusingly highlighted the inventiveness of the State Department travel agency. Shortly after arriving in Estonia, Dave was summoned to a meeting at the European Command post for US forces in Stuttgart, Germany. As he got to the airport outside of Tallinn, he and the military attachés were escorted to the chartered plane. As he was about to board, he stepped back as his initial astonishment went from disbelief to pure amusement.

"The State Department located a private plane for me to charter, and on the tail, it said 'Moscow Golf Club'! The military attachés didn't know what to say. I didn't know what to say. It had been cleared by the State Department. When we landed at the military airport in Germany, our reception committee started laughing. Even the Russian pilots were laughing," recounted Dave. It seems that the irony of the situation was just so extremely odd that the only reaction was laughter, the universal language. Dave still laughs as he recalls the story.

Another story recalled by Dave proves the saying, "It's a small world after all," to be more than an axiom. Offices of the FBI are located throughout the world, and the Estonia FBI Office was the first to host the European Leadership Conference in a former Soviet Union country. Dave welcomed the FBI director, Robert Mueller, to Estonia, and he was accompanied by the FBI assistant director, Louis F. Quijas. Quijas was the former police chief in the Phillips's hometown of High Point, North Carolina.

After the opening ceremony, the FBI legal attachés gathered outside of the Olympia Hotel for a group photograph. No one realized that they were posing underneath a sign, in big letters, of the restaurant's name, ironically "Bonnie and Clyde." The restaurant had been built by the Soviets for the 1980 Olympics when Estonia hosted the sailing competition. The United States did not participate in the 1980 Olympics because President Carter called upon the Olympic Committee to boycott the Games due to the Soviet invasion of Afghanistan.

Dave's experience in both politics and business served him well while he was an ambassador in Estonia. Every five years, each of the US embassies in the world is visited by an evaluation team from the Inspector General's Office. The duty of the team was to interview everyone in the US Embassy. The scope of their appraisal extended beyond auditing the work and financial aspects, delving also into the professional dynamics of the staff. The team needed to know how the staff dealt with all facets of their designated country, in this case, Estonia.

The team leaders who came to Estonia were three retired career ambassadors. Dave noted, "After spending many days at the Embassy and in our home, they asked me, 'What do you see as your role here?' I told them, 'I see myself as a salesman. My job is to sell America. Every country in the world is considered a sales territory. Every country in the world should learn the products of America: independence, democracy, and capitalism. The president of America is the CEO, the citizens of America are the shareholders, the secretary of state is the international sales manager, and I am the salesman to Estonia.' These three men from the Inspector General's Office just looked at me and said, 'We have never, ever heard anyone say that before.'"

At the time, Dave admitted, "I didn't know if they thought it was good or bad. I couldn't believe that it just poured out of my mouth. I wondered if other ambassadors felt the same way."

In one of his first interviews, on May 15, 2007, with Erkki Bahovski of *Postimees*, Dave was asked, "What are your priorities in Estonia?" He answered, "I am a businessman, and that has been my major experience in life. I would like to find ways that would help Estonia and the United States do business together. Also, my wife and I are involved in several cultural projects in America, and we would like to support exchanges between our two countries."

In another 2007 interview, this time for the *Narvskaya Gazeta*, a local Russian-language newspaper, just a few months after his arrival, Dave spoke of his job as ambassador, "No two days are alike. A day starts with an overview of Estonian media that includes topics from all of the newspapers translated from Estonian and Russian."

When asked in an interview what the United States means to Estonia, Dave replied, "Estonia is a symbol of what a country can do in today's world.

Not only has Estonia achieved great success, it is also leading the way for other countries that strive for independence. Estonia is highly regarded, thanks to your accomplishments in information technology. Internet banking and e-government has made your country known as 'E-stonia.'"

This quote was made in reference to Estonia's emergence as a paperless society, one of the most advanced e-societies in the world at the time. E-services in Estonia include e-elections, e-taxes, e-healthcare, e-banking, e-school, and e-government. Almost any activity could be taken care of over the internet in just a few clicks, and that was in 2007.

One of the most memorable experiences while serving in Estonia emerged from the Phillips's previous involvement in the Special Olympics World Games. Since Dave had served as the chairman of the 1999 Special Olympics, both he and Kay developed a deep and affectionate fondness for Special Olympians. They also maintained a friendship with Sargent Shriver, chairman of the Special Olympics. Kay and Dave inquired of the Estonians if there were any Estonian athletes who would be participating in the World Games in China in 2007. They were delighted to hear that Estonia would be sending a delegation to Shanghai, China, for the competition. Kay and Dave were deeply appreciative and honored at what happened next.

The delegation asked Kay if she would walk in the opening ceremony in Shanghai with the Estonian special athletes. She had already become friends with these special children, and this was an honor that was truly overwhelming, said Dave. Proudly and graciously, Kay walked into the Shanghai stadium with the Estonian team to the roar of 80,000 cheering fans. Dave recalled his pride as he sat among the crowd and saw the picture of his wife on the huge jumbotron. It was an incredible moment for both Kay and Dave. During their time in Shanghai, Kay and Dave attended the events and met many wonderful personalities, including the leaders of China.

While serving as ambassador, Dave enjoyed many other unique experiences. He had the privilege of being part of a historical trip with the Estonian government officials. When Kay and Dave visited France, they had the opportunity to board and tour the *USS Enterprise*, the first and oldest nuclear aircraft carrier in the naval fleet. It was the first military ship to go into French waters in decades and was on course to go to the Middle East.

They attended a ceremony while on board, and Dave approached Admiral James A. (Sandy) Winnefeld, commander of the Sixth Fleet, who later was appointed vice-chairman of the joint chiefs of staff, and asked forthrightly, "Would you ever consider bringing the *USS Enterprise* into the Baltic?" The admiral answered, "I can't turn this ship around in the Baltic." The massive *USS Enterprise* does not ride the high seas solo but rather is accompanied by a fleet comprised of support vessels. However, the admiral did offer an alternate plan: "I will do you one better when we come back through the Mediterranean from the Gulf in six months. I will give you a call and see if you want to bring some of the Estonian leadership on the *USS Enterprise*."

Six months later, Admiral Winnefeld kept his word and called Dave. A plane was sent to Estonia to transport the Estonian president, Toomas Hendrik Ilves, and the Estonian leadership to the *USS Enterprise* in the Mediterranean Sea. "It was an incredible day. It was the first time a sitting president of any nation had landed on the *USS Enterprise*.

"They changed the laws of Estonia because most of the leadership of the government of Estonia was on board the plane. When we returned, it was feared that if the plane crashed it would have wiped out the leadership of Estonia." Such a situation occurred in Poland several years later.

The experience of landing on an aircraft carrier was very riveting. "It was one of the most incredible experiences you could imagine."

The landing went smoothly and, fortunately, survival techniques were not needed. They spent the day touring the *USS Enterprise* and watching the jets flawlessly land and take off. They visited the command center, were introduced to the various offensive and defensive weapons systems, and were shown the daily life of the 5,000-member crew. The landing had been so smooth that the passengers were unconcerned about the ensuing lift-off, feeling that if there was a disturbance, it surely would have occurred while trying to stop the plane on the limited runway. They were in for a surprise.

Dave explained, "We were told it would be an abrupt stop when we landed. We were prepared, and it was okay. When we took off, we thought we could handle it and were unconcerned at the time. Then the plane took off and dropped dramatically. That is what it is supposed to do, but we didn't know it. We couldn't hear the engines. We couldn't see out of the windows. We were strapped in our seats. Well, you have never heard so many people, including the press, saying that this was the scariest thing they had ever been through. Finally, to our relief, the plane stopped falling, caught the air, and started ascending.

"It had been a spectacular day for Estonia and a magnificent show of force for America."

The Marine Embassy Guards are responsible for guarding the Embassy. One of the "perks" of being on the elite Embassy Security Guard detail is the housing. They live in a private compound. They have their own cook, a well-equipped workout room, a volleyball field, a billiards room, and a well-stocked bar. The bar operated as a for-profit business, and Kay and Dave were known to stop in and sip a few with the marines. "This is where the embassy people hung out. It was private and comfortable. We loved the marines. They are a real focal point for any embassy anywhere in the world. They made us, as Americans, feel so proud. Every year, marines around the world have the famous Marine Ball. Kay and I attend the ball every year."

One of the Marine Balls they attended proved to be even more special and involved a female member of the Estonian military, serving in Afghanistan, whose leg was blown off in combat. Although her leg was gone, her spirits and outlook were terrific. Dave arranged for her to get treatment at Walter Reed in America.

The young lady returned to Estonia that autumn. Dave recalled, "I asked her to be our guest at the annual Marine Ball. The grandeur and uniforms were spectacular as the marines invited their counterparts from other foreign embassies around the world. That year, I had the great honor of delivering the 'welcome' and then asked the young lady for the first dance. It was very emotional."

When I asked Dave what was most memorable about his tenure as ambassador, he leaned back to think about it, and said, "Estonia was the first nation in the world to be attacked by cyberwarfare, and we had the chance and privilege to serve all those people at such an important time. Many people have asked me, 'Weren't you worried being there during that attack?' My answer is no. I wouldn't have wanted it any other way."

# CHAPTER 27

# *Come On, America!*

Dave's appointment as US ambassador to Estonia ended in 2009, and he and Kay were back home at Valleyfields Farm once again.

"In 2010, one year before my fiftieth reunion at Choate," Dave said, "a letter arrived. I was sitting at the breakfast table, opening the mail, and when I opened that letter, I couldn't believe it. I started crying. They were awarding me the Choate Seal. I felt incredibly honored."

Dave would be too humble to tell you this himself, but I did some research, and now it's my turn to brag on Dave a little bit.

In 2010, S. Davis Phillips received the Choate Seal Prize, the highest honor to be bestowed upon an alumnus, an honor reserved for the very few. Others who have received the Choate Seal include its first recipient, John F. Kennedy, along with Adlai Stevenson, Paul Mellon, Edward Albee, Michael Douglas, Ali McGraw, and Glenn Close. The Choate Seal is given for "outstanding leadership and for making significant contributions to their country, community, and school."

In his introduction, Choate Headmaster Edward J. Shanahan described Phillips as a businessman, philanthropist, civic leader, and former North Carolina secretary of commerce who brought tremendous experience to his service as a US ambassador to the Republic of Estonia.

Headmaster Shanahan further explained, "S. Davis Phillips came to Choate in September 1957 from a prominent family in High Point. As the result of a physical handicap, a below-the-knee leg amputation, Dave's participation in sports was limited, but his enthusiasm knew no bounds." He earned varsity letters as co-manager of the football and wrestling teams. Said Coach Burge Ayres of Dave's leadership abilities, "He lifted each team by the enormous force of his personality."

Dave told me that it had been a long time since he had walked the halls as a floundering student, and yet on this day, it seemed he was back home. He could almost hear the footsteps of his headmaster and now friend, Seymour St. John. Unfortunately, St. John died before Dave received this honor, but undoubtedly, he would be proud.

Dave hadn't been a perfect student. He had not even been a good student. He often broke the rules and was suspended for it, but his days at Choate had made an invaluable impact on his future. Many of the lessons of life were not learned through a schoolbook but through Choate's high expectations and their standards of high principles, values, and friendships.

"So, now that you've shared your life with me," I said, "let me ask you a big question: what advice would you give people today, based on your experiences?"

Dave's answer came surprisingly quick. "Well, I'll tell you what I told my family just recently. I turned seventy-six this year. I've lived about one third of America's history. That's hard to fathom.

My whole life, I've been curious about the world, and I'm still curious. Kay and I just returned from visiting Dubai. The tallest building in the world is in Dubai, and it's beautiful. It was designed by an architect from Chicago. The hotel we were staying in was incredible, built to resemble a massive sailing ship in the Persian Gulf. It was designed by an architect from China.

The people of Dubai are so courteous, and they're from all over the world. I had never seen so many people together from diverse places like Africa, India, China, and Russia. I had to ask everyone I met where they were from and why they were there, so I had all sorts of conversations with people at the restaurants, in our hotel, on the street, in the elevator, and in the business district. They couldn't have been nicer as we talked about the world.

I kept looking for Americans, but I saw very few.

It's a whole new mindset, where people from all different cultures and religions are working and living together to build something beautiful. You feel like you're in a modern oasis. And you are. We visited another new city in the United Arab Emirates (UAE): Abu Dhabi. The Louvre in Paris, the greatest museum in the world, has just opened its only branch in the world there. Naturally, the museum is extremely modern and sophisticated.

As I was thinking about how the UAE evolved, I couldn't help but think about how America evolved, too.

I'm worried that we in America don't think about how fortunate we've been, where we've come from, and where we're going. We don't know how to work together. Or we've forgotten."

"Why do you think that is?" I asked.

"Because we don't trust each other. Not very long ago, the FBI was the most trusted institution in America. The top companies on the New York Stock Exchange used to be highly regarded. The news media was an unquestioned source of objective news. Today, we don't trust our government institutions, we don't trust companies, and we don't trust our leaders. We don't even trust the news to tell us what's true.

This lack of public trust worries me because it's the public who participates in capitalism. Capitalism is the backbone of America and democracy itself. It's where people have the opportunity to be successful in their own creation, whether it's a product, a service, or an idea.

The integration of different races and cultures is going to continue at a very fast pace from now on around the world because of our ability to instantly communicate with everyone around the world. And that's what stunned me in Dubai.

America has been slow to appreciate what is happening in the world. It might be because our population is contained by the oceans. But even so, we've got to learn to work together with people who look, act, and believe differently than we do.

For example, we might think of China as a dictatorship, but the truth is, it's pregnant with capitalism.

America is made up of individuals. And every individual goes through adversity in their lives. I don't care if you're rich, poor, black, white, handicapped, star athlete, executive, addict, scholar, or a high school dropout. Our problem is that most people focus on what hasn't gone right for them and whine about it—and miss the unique opportunities for success they do have.

Our challenge as a nation is personal: no matter what adversity we've faced, we need to find the confidence to show up in our lives, look each other in the eye, smile, and start a conversation—even and especially with those who might disagree with us! That's how we're going to rebuild trust in our nation.

It's that simple. Have the confidence to be visible in your real life, not just online. Take an interest in the person standing right next to you. Make a face-to-face connection and remember that no matter what your favorite news source is or who you follow on social media, we're all human beings on the same planet, trying to do the best we can with what we've got.

So, come on America! Find your taste of success and build on it. Thank God for our country, for our freedom, for our democracy, and for capitalism, where everybody has an opportunity for success. We should be an example for the world."

# ACKNOWLEDGMENTS

A very special thanks to Dave Phillips for giving me this special opportunity to write *Come On, America,* my first book. He was so gracious in sharing his incredible life and life's lessons with me. I truly value our indelible friendship.

Another special thank you goes to Amanda Rooker, whose command of the written word helped smooth the manuscript. Her help during this process has been priceless.

And thank you to Morgan James Publishing for all their support during this process.

# ABOUT THE AUTHOR

Mary Bogest is a writer and an artist who enjoys the beauty of North Carolina from the mountains to the ocean. *Come On, America* is her first book. She resides in High Point, North Carolina, with her two adorable dogs, Juliette and Josie.

 Morgan James makes all of our titles available
through the Library for All Charity Organization.

www.LibraryForAll.org